Chasing Cynthiana

Chasing Cynthiana

My Search for America's Native Wines

LYNN HAMILTON

Potomac Books
AN IMPRINT OF THE UNIVERSITY OF NEBRASKA PRESS

Manufactured in the United States of America.

Library of Congress Cataloging-in-Publication Data

Names: Hamilton, Lynn, 1964– author.
Title: Chasing Cynthiana: my search for America's
native wines / Lynn Hamilton.
Description: [Lincoln]: Potomac Books, an imprint of the University
of Nebraska Press, [2024] | Includes bibliographical references.
Identifiers: LCCN 2024019708
ISBN 9781640126176 (hardback)
ISBN 9781640126374 (epub)
ISBN 9781640126381 (pdf)
Subjects: LCSH: Wine industry—United States. | BISAC:
COOKING / Beverages / Alcoholic / Wine | BIOGRAPHY
& AUTOBIOGRAPHY / Personal Memoirs
Classification: LCC HD9375 .H28 2024 | DDC
338.4/766320973—dc23/eng/20240716
LC record available at https://lccn.loc.gov/2024019708

Designed and set in Arno Pro by Scribe Inc.

CONTENTS

PHOTOGRAPHS

Following chapter 4

PREFACE

Some people need to pull off the highway to see Bigfoot at Maine's Cryptozoology Museum. Others need to see a black bear driving a scooter. Sometimes the detours are the best parts of a trip. For me, nothing matches the thrill of pulling off the interstate to find an independent winery.

The subculture of American wine tasting is ever evolving. Those of us who venture into the world of local wines, who avidly sample the fiercely uncool apple and cherry wines made from local fruit, must prepare for frequent disappointment. This world produces many wines that are too sweet, marketed too young, or just poorly crafted. The thrill comes from that rare vintage that has eluded every wine publication but still enraptures the drinker with its complexity and mystery.

I don't need a penthouse. I don't need a Tesla. I don't need Armani. What I need is to sit at a table on the edge of a farm while someone refills my wineglass and chats with me about wine. Holding a glass stem, gazing off into the distance where the vine rows give way to a dappled sky, growing slightly buzzed, perhaps taking the hand of my life partner and remembering why we fell in love: this is my idea of wealth and leisure.

We know who we are: we few, we happy few, who see a sign for a vineyard or winery and take the detour. We take that chance. Every time, it's a leap of faith. The destination might be six or seven minutes off the highway, or it might take us down farm roads, through ten or more turns, and half an hour off the safe tar and stripes of the interstate.

That's not the only risk. There's also the risk that the wine will suck. That no matter how many varietals we try, no matter how assiduously we read the menu and ask questions, there will be no justification for this trip.

We try to find at least one taste we like. It might be the cranberry Chardonnay or the plum medley. It's usually safer to lean into the fruity, dessert-y products. Making a good dry wine is an expert-level skill, and many small wineries simply don't have the "it" that makes a good dry wine.

Still, we persist, stubbornly Voltairean in our expectations. If we do not see something pleasant, at least we will see something new. There's another sign, this one for Hunter's Bluff Winery, and we take a chance. Because every winery is like traveling to a foreign country. We pan for a good wine, like prospectors of the wild Northwest.

I'm not a wine connoisseur. I'm not a wine snob. I'm a wine lover. Or at least, I try to be. In fact, few wines are actually loveable. I can down a decent Merlot or Prosecco with dinner, and mostly, I like the wines I order or find in a store. Even more rarely do I find something to love at a local winery, but the search is rife with adventure. And, once in a while, there is a wine to love.

In 2006, I discovered such a wine at Three Sisters, a north Georgia vineyard and winery. It was made from a grape called Cynthiana, or Norton, depending on where you are drinking it. Cynthiana wasn't just a good wine; it was a revelation. The grape is grown right in north Georgia. I would eventually discover that it can be grown almost everywhere. And the Norton/Cynthiana grape was hybridized right off a wild American grape in the nineteenth century. My first response, shooting straight off my id, was *Where do I get more?* The next question, asked by my inner writer, was *And why am I just now hearing about this?* I have no actual wine training, but I've been sampling and chugging wine for my entire adulthood, asking questions of people who know more than me, and doing a little informal research.

And yet, no one had ever told me about Cynthiana. It radically changed my ideas about the wine landscape in America. This is a wine that can be grown in the United States, outside California. It not only grows but thrives. It got me thinking about wine snobbery and the assumption of many winemakers and wine drinkers that the good wine is all made in California and Europe.

The American wine industry outside California has lagged behind Europe's for far too long for reasons that have little to do with actual taste or quality. The disruption caused by Prohibition is only part of the problem. U.S. wine dealers are biased against wine made outside the wine regions that have immediate name recognition. Some great American wines will never get that name recognition because dealers and distributors never introduce consumers to wines that fall outside their comfort zones. There's a closed loop in wine sales that is very difficult for a new American winemaker growing outside California to penetrate.

Several wine merchants have explained to me that their customers will not like a wine made outside Europe or California. And many American wine drinkers also imagine that the only good wines are made in Europe and California, which perpetuates the cycle of wariness by U.S. wine retailers. As a consequence, Americans are largely uneducated about their own wine history. For example, few Americans know anything about their native grapes: *Vitis aestivalis* and *Vitis labrusca*.

Studies of U.S. wine tend to focus on California, with narratives like the Judgment of Paris ennobling the bootstrapping nature of America's wines. But the true bootstrappers are the scrappy winemakers in Wisconsin, Missouri, Arkansas, Virginia, and Georgia. Some U.S. wineries produce such good wine that the product is entirely bought out by local wine drinkers and visitors, often not even making it to the local restaurants. It is time wine made from U.S. native grapes came into its own.

Chasing Cynthiana

1

Fat Boy to Cynthiana

Back in 2006, I went to a wine festival in the mountains of north Georgia. And, yes, I know you're thinking of *Deliverance* and "Dueling Banjos." But the hilly area an hour or two west of Atlanta is more suburban than you think and getting more so every day. There I was, a middle-aged cliché: visor, capri pants, smeared in sunscreen, all pastelled up for a warm, bright day. The other wine tasters were just about as unfashionable and similarly restrained.

The wine wasn't flowing. It was coming out in short, frustrating burps from bottles that had been handicapped with those stoppers that regulate each pour to an ounce or less. No one was getting drunk here or even loosening their grasp on the real. The samples ranged in quality from tasty enough in very small doses to nasty enough to be glad you didn't get more. Few, if any, bottles were leaving the festival.

The vendors were working hard and fast, getting a little harried. Their mornings had started out at five or six. They had to load the table and the wines into their trucks and drive to this remote location where they then unloaded and set up. No one ever claimed that tabling is easy work. They were making sure no one got more than she paid for. They were cold sober and probably longing for their couches, their flat screens, and the expiation of their sins in church the next day.

But there, on the outer edge of the festival, was a table where people were having fun. I approached. The vendor was wearing a shirt with the image of a healthy farm pig that said "Fat Boy." It was stained with a recent wine spill. He didn't care that his shirt was stained. He was visibly buzzed on his own product and regaling anyone who dropped by.

He was free pouring, having removed the sample stopper—or perhaps he never put it on to begin with. From this young man, I learned that Fat Boy was a red blend, the basis of which was the Cynthiana grape. The company making that wine was a family-owned vineyard and winery called Three Sisters, located about eleven miles due north of Dahlonega, Georgia.

I tried his wine. It was quite good, much better than the other varietals that had dutifully shown up for this festival. Stumbling upon Cynthiana this way was a bit like wandering through a sidewalk art fair with low expectations and then realizing that Michelangelo had set up a booth, for some unfathomable reason, and was selling originals of Adam, fresh out of his creation story, gorgeously naked with all his muscles in the right places.

I left with a crate of Fat Boy, which didn't last long at our cabin in the woods, where the nearest full grocery was a thirty-minute drive away. From that moment, I was on a near-constant quest to locate the next bottle of this novel vintage. Some restaurants had it—most did not. I plugged it mercilessly to overworked bartenders: "If you're looking for a new wine to add to your list, please consider Three Sisters and Fat Boy!"

Proving that the wonder of life prevails, the downtown Blue Ridge independent bookstore sold local wines. The owner had a small but decent collection of books, mostly vintage, and he discreetly sold vintage firearms as well, but you had to know about the guns to see the guns. When the store passed from him to a younger entrepreneur, it became substantially more mainstream, specializing in popular paperbacks, especially science fiction. It also became substantially less fun. No more literary curveballs. No more wine sales, and the new owner complains that the Bureau of Alcohol, Tobacco, Firearms and Explosives still visits him to make sure he's not selling weapons.

From the former owner, however, I bought a hardback Garrison Keillor story collection and, hallelujah, a bottle of Fat Boy. From this knowledgeable local, I also learned that Three Sisters had produced a mother wine, called simply Cynthiana, after their main grape. It was a pure, unblended vintage. Could I buy a bottle of that? No, I could not. The vineyard was sold out for the season.

I happened on it, though, at a restaurant called Harvest on Main, which specializes in getting its food from local growers. Harvest is particularly popular with north Georgia's day-trippers and the leaf lookers who come in October to see the fall foliage. There is often a line and a wait for the restaurant's main dining room. But, on this particular afternoon, we got in right away.

There, on the wine list, was Cynthiana. Did the restaurant really have some in stock? Yes, it did. Under Harvest's half-timbered, high ceiling, where each heavy table reminds diners that tables come from trees, I drank my first bottle of Cynthiana. And so it began.

It was even better than Fat Boy. Like a few other really good red wines, the Three Sisters' Cynthiana paired well with everything I ate, right through to and including the chocolate course. The wine also had "it," that ineffable thing that a good wine has. Wine drinkers have agreed on a vocabulary that includes phrases like *legs, texture, complexity, velvety, balance, layers, notes of vanilla, notes of cinnamon,* and so on. These are all attempts to describe what happens when we drink a good glass of wine.

When the wine is really, really good, it opens a door in your brain and lets in the mild euphoria. Nothing manic. Nothing that endangers your balance or makes Mr. Wrong look like the love of your life. That's bourbon. Wine, drunk in moderation, offers only a gentle derangement. This Cynthiana had all the things: dimensions, different forward and aftertastes, the capacity to turn a plain woman into a poet.

I had, for days, been struggling to lower my blood pressure. The med tech who was supposed to call in my prescription had dropped the ball. I had been on the phone that morning yelling at the pharmacy, yelling at the clinic's answering service. But when I got home from that lunch, I took my blood pressure. It had gone down fifty points to a normal range.

Okay, that might be too much of a claim for a half bottle of wine. Nevertheless, it cannot have been my imagination entirely that Cynthiana has, among other things, health benefits. A 2012 study conducted by Chinese scientists in Beijing looks at the quantities of healthful phenolic components in wines. It will come as no surprise to many readers that red wines are higher in these substances than white or rose wines.[1]

Where this gets interesting is that Lei Zhu and his colleagues at China Agricultural University found that Cynthiana has the highest concentrations of phenols, including anthocyanins, flavonols, and phenolic acids, as well as antioxidants of all the red wines. The second richest in these nutrients is Chambourcin. Merlot and Cabernet Sauvignon have the lowest amounts.[2] (Yes, they were growing Cynthiana in China. Might they know something?)

And why should phenols matter? Phenolic compounds, found naturally in many plants, may help humans fend off cancer, heart disease, and diabetes, to name the most prevalent and catastrophic diseases. The next year, 2007, I went back directly to Three Sisters, early in the season, and bought a crate of Cynthiana.

I am not alone in falling in love with a wine that, in its infancy, was nicknamed the "Virginia seedling." Paul Roberts, whose love of this wine drove him to establish his own vineyard and winery in Maryland, came back from a trip from France, where his relish for a La Lagune turned him into a wine lover. When he tasted a Cynthiana from Missouri, it turned him into a wine yearner: "It was rich and intensely flavored and oozing with unusual coffee and berry smells. Wow! What nerve! I eyed the wine in that glass the way one contemplates a heckler," he writes.[3]

To the open mind, life is a fun classroom, and wines come in many colors and tastes. But my mind and taste buds keep drifting back to Cynthiana. Is it really America's only really good native wine grape? Who grows it? And where can I get the next bottle? I have been chasing Cynthiana, in amateur fashion, for years, and now, it's time to chase it in earnest.

2

Origins of Cynthiana

I'm not going to bury the lead here. Norton wine and Cynthiana wine are made from the same grape. At the end of the day, they are the same wine varietal. This one wine has two different names, several different regions, merging fan clubs, and two origin stories.

In Missouri, which has the strongest historical claim to the grape, it is called Norton, and in Arkansas, it is mostly called Cynthiana. Elsewhere, the naming of this wine is a crapshoot. In Kentucky, for instance, most wineries call it Norton. In Virginia, where Jennifer McCloud reintroduced the vintage, she ran with the Missouri nomenclature, Norton. And her many protégés followed suit. At Three Sisters, the oldest vineyard in north Georgia, they ran with the name Cynthiana.

Despite solid, peer-reviewed DNA evidence, a few enthusiasts persist in believing that one wine is two wines. I am not here to argue with the experts. For the purposes of this book, though, I am assuming that Norton and Cynthiana come from the same species of grape.

It would be remiss to give the impression that all Cynthiana and Norton wines taste the same just because they have the same grape DNA. That is not the case. To say that two grapes have the same DNA tells us nothing about the quality of the wine.

Even the most casual wine bibbers can tell the difference between a good Cabernet and a Cabernet mass-produced for cheapness and quantity. A decent rule of thumb: if a wine is presented in overly large bottles or boxes, it's a good bet that it's a cheap and mediocre wine. Winemakers with any pretensions to seriousness mostly present their product in 750-milliliter bottles. Wine is only at peak condition for about twenty hours after being opened, so the five-glass bottle is convenient for couples who wish to each drink two fair-sized glasses of wine with dinner or who wish to carefully stretch their bottle over two dinners, imbibing only a glass and a quarter each at each meal.

However, the 750-milliliter bottle is tradition; the bottle does not make the wine. Also, there are exceptions. Sofia Coppola, for instance, makes a fully decent (and affordable!) Blanc in a can. Some mid-budget French winemakers present decent wines in larger bottles that may work well for extended families and small dinner parties.

A hundred or so factors go into making a quality wine. The grapes have to be grown with tender loving care, the soil quality matters, which vines are nurtured and which are deselected matters, hybridization matters, cloning matters. And that's all before we get to the weather, which can ruin a wine in one bad summer week before it gets anywhere close to the laboratory.

When grapes are cultivated with all the best care that science and tradition dictate, then the winemaker takes over as the make-or-break factor. How the juice is extracted, what barrels it is stored in, how long it is aged and at what temperature, and how it is stoppered all play a part in making a wine good or bad.

The Norton grape is the basis of a delicious wine, but it can be ruined at an almost unlimited number of points in its timeline. I have personally tasted some unbelievably bad Norton wine, and some heavenly Norton wine. Tolstoy's rule about families—the happy ones are all the same, the miserable ones all unique—applies to wine. A good Cynthiana/Norton will taste similar to another good Cynthiana/Norton, but the bad ones are all differently bad. A bad Norton wine is as different from a good Norton wine as Gatorade is different from Prosecco.

Norton grapes and wine take the name of Dr. Daniel Norton, a Virginian of the 1800s. Like the founding fathers, especially Thomas Jefferson and George Washington, he was a Renaissance man—a physician by trade but also fascinated with science, especially as applied to agriculture. Norton's story is infused with sadness, however. He lost his biological father at the age of three, and his mother, Catherine Bush, remarried two years later. She married the wealthy Virginia delegate and militia veteran John Ambler.

This marriage had two opposing effects: it sheltered and protected Catherine and her son—Norton was raised alongside his half siblings—but Norton felt keenly that Ambler's own children received more consideration. Upon reaching adulthood, Norton received a gift of slaves who had belonged to his biological father, but one of Ambler's biological children received an entire plantation. Daniel Norton was plagued by a belief that he had been robbed of an undefined birthright at the same time that he declared himself too proud to ask the Amblers for help.

He attended medical school and became a doctor but did not rise to distinction in that profession. In the early 1800s, medicine was not held in the esteem in which it is held today. Law and politics were much more prestigious fields.

If Norton ever had any passion for doctoring, it quickly gave way to cynicism. He came to call himself a "Pill Garlick." This delightful term, roughly meaning "blockhead," has fallen out of use, but it refers to Edmund Temple's 1813 novel *The Life of Pill Garlick*. At the time Temple appropriated the term, it was already in currency as a sobriquet for a man of little intelligence, low drive, poor judgment, and embarrassing adventures related to the first three attributes. "Pill Garlick" also and sometimes simultaneously referred to a bald man, one whose pate looked like peeled garlic.

A happy marriage and the expectation of his first child briefly cheered Norton. Then he lost both his beloved wife and the couple's first child in labor. A pall of melancholy descended on the good doctor. Today, we would say his hereditary inclination to depression was triggered by the loss. Norton found solace in farming. The passion that medicine failed to inspire would be found within the work of viniculture, which he pursued on his Magnolia Farm.

The year was 1821. The country was new, invention was the prerogative of the gentleman farmer, Washington had devised a vaccine against smallpox, Jefferson had invented the moldboard plow. It was a world of opportunity, a place where everything could be reimagined and made better.

It was the destiny of landowners to make agriculture more efficient and exciting. Like his country's founders, Norton avidly read all the new articles about agricultural science and the new tools. Why should a nation that had thrown off so many shackles of pointless tradition not have its own new-and-improved wine? It was a question worth asking, and Norton sought to answer it.

Legend has it that, under a cloud of sadness, but also prepared to find something amazing, Norton was surveying his grounds, and he saw a healthy and unusual cluster of grapes. They were a dark, dark purple, blackish. Norton concluded that this was not an old-world grape but a hybrid of *Vitis vinifera,* a European grape species, and *Vitis labrusca,* a grape native to North America. The hybridization of these species would have solved several problems that had heretofore plagued American winemaking.

The old-world *vinifera* is the basis of most European wine grapes, and when Norton discovered his namesake grape, American winemakers had been trying to grow this *Vitis vinifera* literally for two hundred years, with almost no success. It was very hard to grow in the eastern United States. *Vinifera's* delicate grapes could not withstand the punishing hot summers or the cold, cold winters of the colonies. Meanwhile, several species of grape are native to North America, and these grapes grow wild, survive cold winters and punishingly hot summers. The most important North American species are the sweet and foxy *Vitis labrusca* and the dry, mysterious *Vitis aestivalis.* Wine can be made from both these grapes, either in pure or in hybrid form. But, until Daniel Norton bottled wine from *Vitis aestivalis,* no one seriously thought that good wine could be made from a native American grape.

The lack of wine grapes was a sticking point for Virginia. Attitudes toward alcoholic beverages have changed often over the centuries, but the colonists considered wine more or less an inalienable right. It was an outrage that the New World, which offered delicious growing soil for food and tobacco, could not cough up a fermentable grape.

Virginia was so desperate for wine that, at one point, all householders were required by law to grow a quantum of grapes on their property, "on paine of death," if they refused.[1] This experiment failed miserably, as did all other early attempts to grow European grapes on American soil. Exasperated American farmers of the nineteenth century, railroaded into growing grapes they didn't want, threw their grape-growing manuals in the fire to keep warm during a particularly brutal Virginia winter.

As the wise William Penn (also a wine drinker interested in viniculture) notes about plants, "Not only a thing groweth best, where it naturally grows; but will hardly be equalled by another species of the same kind, that doth not naturally grow there."[2] *Vitis vinifera* really, really didn't want to grow on America's East Coast or in the Midwest. It would eventually grow in California. In the twentieth and twenty-first centuries, new grape-growing technologies have made it possible to grow European grapes in other states, but there are still challenges.

Norton, who can truly be called the unsung father of American wine, would pioneer the method of grafting *vinifera* vines onto native American grapevine roots, and that is one of the reasons that Virginia can produce Chardonnays and Cabernets today. When he discovered his new grape species, Norton believed that his attempt to hybridize the native *Vitis labrusca* onto the European grape, *Vitis vinifera*, had succeeded. (It would turn out he was at least partly mistaken about the parentage of the Norton seedling. More on that later.)

Nothing could be more different from *vinifera* than *Vitis labrusca* and still call itself a grape. In the early 1800s, American wine enthusiasts were already well familiar with *Vitis labrusca*, a sturdy grape that was growing wild across a wide swathe of North America when the Pilgrims got off their boats.

It may have been discovered by Leif Ericsson, the Norse explorer who took a walk in North America about five hundred years before Columbus stumbled upon it.

Vitis labrusca was definitely cataloged by the famed botanist Carl Linneas. It is a round, sweet grape that gives us those delicious Concord table grapes as well as grape juice and jelly. *Labrusca* is a wonderful grape, but does it make a decent wine? Purists adamantly say, "No, too foxy." Foxiness in wines can really only fully be understood by the indomitable off-interstate wine tasters. (See the preface.) From tasting many wines made with Niagara grapes, Catawba grapes, and Muscadines, we know fox, and words will always fail to translate it to those whose wine experience has not ventured past the package store.

Foxiness in wine is not bad, per se, but it's different from your California Cabernet. Foxy wines taste simultaneously rawer, fruitier, and more powdery, definitely less nuanced. Foxy wines taste more like the skin of the grape than the pulp. Fox might be the equivalent of "gaminess" in meat; it's a wilder, less cultivated taste. Like something you found or shot in a forest rather than something raised on a farm.

Why in heaven's name did we land on the word *fox* to describe this phenomenon? Well, the answer is that "fox grape" is the nickname for *Vitis labrusca*. Fox, as a wine trait, is inexorably tied to *Vitis labrusca*, which is the foxiest grape of them all.

Norton believed that the new hybrid grape, which would come to bear his name, was a *Vitis labrusca* varietal called Bland. Norton remembered planting Bland and pollinating it with the old-world *Vitis vinifera*. However, recent DNA tests neither confirm nor deny that the lost Bland can be found anywhere in the markers of the current Norton grape.

To return, then, to the hybrid grape found by Norton in 1821, DNA tests have shown that a major part of its makeup is *Vitis aestivalis*, a wild grape around which there is still an aura of mystery. The Cherokees knew all about the native *aestivalis* grape and used it in their ceremonies. It was also an ingredient in antidiarrheal treatments.

Wine experts generally agree that *Vitis aestivalis* makes a better wine than *labrusca*. *Aestivalis* has a good profile of tannins and is much less foxy than other wild North American grapes. As all native plants do where they are native, it holds up well in North American soil and doesn't languish in our weather. But it is hard to propagate from cuttings. *Vitis aestivalis* dominates the makeup of Norton/Cynthiana, according to recent DNA tests.

With a shaky understanding of what he had grown, but complete confidence that he had grown it, Daniel Norton picked the berries of this new grape. He pressed them and bottled the juice, aged it a few months, and then sampled. It was better than he expected. His mind drifted to the French Bordeaux, a similar wine, he thought. Kliman writes, "He did not yet know that he had cracked the code,"[3] meaning he had accomplished what no American winemaker had accomplished during two hundred years of colonial life: make a truly fine red wine from grapes grown in the United States.

Norton suspected himself of greatness, and he sent a vine of the new grape to William Prince Jr., whose family managed a huge botanical and educational garden called the Linnaean Botanic Garden. This garden was, for some time, the biggest purveyor of fruit trees and grapevines in the country. Prince would soon establish himself as an expert in American horticulture by writing and publishing *A Short Treatise on Horticulture* (1828), which is widely regarded as the first authoritative book in its field.

Norton wisely understood that he was helpless to market a new wine, much less a new wine grape, without the help of the Princes, who also published a catalog of plants. For farmers and gardeners growing food in the 1800s in America, this book held the same importance as the internet holds for today's growers. It provided an inventory of the Princes' products while also introducing new and interesting plants, with descriptions. The Prince family's acknowledgment of the new grape would mean everything to Norton. If the good doctor were ever to shake off his obscurity, it would be due to the Prince catalog.

So the new grapevine made its way to the Princes' farm, and in 1822, they dubbed it "Norton's Virginia Seedling." In 1830, they would bestow it with the more ostentatious Latin name, *Vitis nortoni*.

Norton found the recognition that had eluded him in medicine. And though he did not live to see old age, he did find happiness with a second wife, Lucy Marshall Fisher. They married in 1831, after a somewhat whirlwind romance—their engagement was a mere four months. They had five children together over the ensuing years.

In 1833, musicians and actors did not often tremble in their boots over the possibility of bad national press, but horticulturists did. There were a surprising number of agricultural journals with distributions roughly equivalent to today's *Rolling Stone*.

Norton received and weathered a bad review of *Vitis nortoni* in the widely read *American Farmer*. The magazine's editor, Gideon B. Smith, had received a sample of the raw grapes and found them "harsh" tasting. Kliman has thrown some shade on Smith, questioning whether he bothered to discern that these were wine grapes and not meant for the table. He has also questioned whether the grapes Smith reviewed were even Norton grapes.[4]

For his part, Norton stood by his grape. When the *Farmer's Register* picked up the *American Farmer* review, he sensed the potential damage of this now viral gossip. He swung into action, sent the *Farmer's Register* a sample of his grape, and asked them to please make their own judgment, rather than relying on secondhand news. His letter made a bold claim: "If the culture of these fruits is attended to, the United States in a few years will cease to import wine."[5]

The response was tepid and ambiguous. The *Farmer's Register* did agree that America needed its own wine industry. In fact, the absence of a decent American wine was declared a national emergency: "We fully believe that the extensive production of pure and unadulterated wine in any country is one of the surest safeguards against drunkenness being a national, or prevailing, vice."[6] (With wine approaching the moral value of the Bible, one *must* wonder what happened between the 1830s and Prohibition.) But the upstart Norton grape was not the answer to the prayers of a nation for a "pure" specimen of wine grape, the editors concluded.

Norton shot back a more specific defense of his grape. He had tried for years to grow old-world grapes, with no success. These attempts had left him with an "empty purse." (His experience mirrored that of everyone else who had attempted to grow fragile European grapes in the hostile U.S. climate.) By contrast, these new grapes all ripened at the same time and were utterly resistant to rot and mildew. Furthermore, wine made from the Norton grape "is luscious beyond anything you can conceive" and had been compared to the Lacryma Christi of Mount Vesuvius.[7]

In comparing his wine to the tears of Jesus, Norton might have been reaching, but no one can fault his conviction. He added words that, in our day, basically mean "This is going to make us rich quick": the Norton grape, he wrote, "properly cultivated, will, at no distant period, be a nucleus whence will emanate an advantage in our exports, scarcely to be calculated."[8]

The secret to a good review turned out to be the wine itself, not the raw grapes. Norton sent a bottle of his wine to yet another farming publication, the *Farmer & Gardener*, and finally, someone got it. The wine was solid, that publication noted: "We do, in all candor affirm, that we consider it a better article than one half of the newfangled liquors which we receive from Europe bearing the name of wine."[9] Translation: "We don't pretend to know anything about wine, but we know what we like."

Whether or not the *Farmer & Gardener* article was the decisive factor, farmers and gardeners started buying Norton seedlings and planting them, with obvious hopes of making a decent home brew. The vines traveled all over the United States, as far west as Ohio, Missouri, and Arkansas, which are still the bastions of Norton wine.

Alas, Norton would not live long enough to fully capitalize on the success of his vintage. He would not reach old age, surrounded by grandchildren. Instead, he would get an unbecoming case of dysentery—that is, violent diarrhea, almost certainly caused by contaminated food or water—from which he would not recover. He died in 1842 at the unripe age of forty-seven. Norton was the most persuasive and tireless advocate for the Norton grape. Who knows what heights of fame the Norton seedling might have reached had he lived to seventy to promote it.

Two years after Norton's death, William Kendrick published his *New American Orchardist*. It turned out that Kendrick had sampled the Norton grape and its wine on a visit to Richmond, Virginia. He had high praise for the fruit, noting its versatility. It made a "good" raw grape for the table, he declared, and an "excellent" wine.[10]

Kendrick had also received a letter directly from Daniel Norton, which claimed that the wine was a hybrid of Bland and Meunier. From the grave, Norton touted the grape's resistance to the "greatest degree of cold which happens in any portion of the union." It was also a low-maintenance grape, Norton averred, "thriving with little care, and never failing to produce abundant crops of fruit."[11]

The Norton could be grown in any state of the union, Norton stated, then backpedaled a little, saying that it could be grown anywhere that Hickory and Oak trees grow. Norton wine was just as good as that stuff they make in France and Madeira, he went on to say. Then, with the American's everlasting assumed privilege to look down on France, he added that, if the French only understood the Norton, it could replace much of that country's "useless trash."[12] In fact, sending American grapes to France would be a terrible and costly mistake. In the 1850s, when American vines did travel to France, they brought the phylloxera insect, which proceeded to decimate vineyards all over Europe. American vines had withstood the phylloxera, but the more fragile *Vitis vinifera* could not. Penn was right. Plant natives.

After Norton's death, the Norton grape narrative received a challenge that wine historians have been fussing about for over a century. The notable Virginian F. W. Lemosy claimed that his father had discovered the grape while shooting ducks on Cedar Island, near Richmond. Lemosy's story contains many realistic details. His father had eaten wild grapes while hunting. When the senior Lemosy brought the grapes home for his family to try, his wife liked them, and they reminded her of some grapes grown in southern France.

After that, Lemosy and his brother went to Cedar Island and gathered those grapes every year. The Lemosy family was friends with Dr. Norton, they introduced him to the grape, and Norton cultivated it. There's a hint, but only a hint, of stolen valor in the words "Dr. Norton developed this grape, and produced a very fine wine; and as he took more interest in it than anyone else, we universally called it Norton's grape . . . by which name I speak of it to this day from mere habit."[13]

Was Lemosy seriously attempting to appropriate Norton's thunder? Taking advantage of Norton's early death to steal the spotlight? The Lemosy family was well known and respected in Richmond. Why would they risk their social standing with a flagrant and self-serving lie?

The alternate Norton grape discovery gained some traction at the time but has been subsequently discredited because the timeline is wrong. Lemosy claimed that his father discovered the grape in 1835 or 1836, but Norton's Virginia Seedling had been listed in the Prince catalog in 1822 and listed again as *Vitis nortoni* in 1830. By 1833, it had already received that damning review in *American Farmer*. So Lemosy's story is definitely inaccurate.

But here's the problem. Norton's own narrative is badly flawed; he seems not to have understood that his grape, the grape named for him, was substantially composed of the wild grape *Vitis aestivalis*. In writing about the grape, he maintained that it was a hybrid of "Bland," an evolution of *Vitis labrusca*, and Meunier, a European wine, and all European wines evolved from *Vitis vinifera*.

Several DNA analyses of the Norton grape have confirmed that it is a combination of *vinifera* and *aestivalis*. A 2010 U.S. Department of Agriculture

(USDA) study did find that there are highly unusual gene markers in Norton that can only be traced to an obscure wine called Enfariné Noir, a relative of the Pinot Meunier that Norton claimed to have hybridized.

The confusion of Enfariné Noir and Pinot Meunier could easily be explained by the parallel evolution of European wines and Norton wine over two hundred years. What is more noticeably missing from the current DNA studies is anything like Bland. The USDA scientists did not want to say that Bland is not in evidence because Bland has disappeared from wine culture altogether. Therefore, there is no way to compare Bland to the current Norton grape. But there's also no evidence that the Norton grape is anything but *vinifera* and *aestivalis*.[14]

Also, there's the taste test. Some Norton wines are plain bad, but not foxy. And wines made from the Bland ancestor, *Vitis labrusca*, are invariably foxy, even when carefully cultivated away from their fox nature. An interview with Jim Lapsley, a University of California wine historian, suggests this possibility: "The introduction of *vinifera*, although unsuccessful, did introduce *vinifera* pollen, which created chance hybrids with the native varieties. These hybrids tasted better—or at least, more like vinifera."[15]

Dr. Norton had planted many grapevines. Could he have mistaken a volunteer hybrid for something he had actually planted? He believed the Norton to be a hybrid he had cultivated, but what if he simply stumbled on a wild grape that had been pollinated by one of the many grapes of European ancestry that he had cultivated?

This theory, if we like it, explains both Norton's and Lemosy's stories. Norton planted *vinifera*, then Norton found a wild grape that had been pollinated by *vinifera*. Years later, Lemosy also found a wild, native grape that had been pollinated by *vinifera*, very likely from Norton's farm. Lemosy may well have sent a bunch of grapes or even a vine to Norton as a curiosity. Then, as people do, he made Norton's story about himself and his grape discovery. Perhaps the latent Pollyanna in me has not been entirely pummeled into nonexistence. For some reason, I don't want either gentleman to be lying, just mistaken.

Both Norton's narrative and Lemosy's narrative contain elements of apparent truth with obvious notes of inaccuracy. In his 1908 book *Grapes of New*

York, Ulysses Prentiss Hedrick seeks to set the record straight. Noting the date that the Prince farm had first received the Norton seedling, he writes that Lemosy's story is "evidently wrong as to dates" and "suspicious as to facts." Nevertheless, he finds it impossible to fully endorse Norton's story either. "It is probable that the true history of the variety will never be known," Hedrick writes,[16] and even DNA evidence has not proven him wrong.

Conflicting origin stories notwithstanding, the grape known as the Virginia seedling and Norton wine continued to be made in Virginia with quite a bit of success. An 1887 article in the *Southern Bivouac* reports that Virginia's winemaking had flourished in the last fifteen years. The author, John S. Gibbs, reports that the grapes grown there included Cynthiana, Concord, Delaware, Hartford, Prolific, Ive's Seedling, Herebemont, Alby, Iona, Diana, Isabella, Clinton, Israella, Catawba, and Norton's Virginia. "The grape entitled to most consideration," Gibbs goes on to say, "and which will eventually win its way every place that it can once get a foothold, is the Norton's Virginia,"[17] which he likens to a French Burgundy. Gibbs tells an interesting story about some Norton that had accidentally gotten aged and served at a party. Everyone who sampled it declared it delicious: "The aging process had so mellowed and softened it as to be truly superb."[18] Gibbs finishes up his article by predicting that the Norton will push out both the mint julep and "John Barleycorn" as a favorite drink of Americans; "this of itself is cause for gratulation."[19]

From Virginia, the Norton grape story takes a leap to Missouri, where struggling Germans immigrated in droves during the 1830s. To understand why so many Germans wanted to leave their fatherland, we have to dive into the history of that country.

The economically thriving and diverse Germany of today shows few, if any, signs of the poverty and crowding that Germany suffered in the early nineteenth century. All over Europe, the Industrial Revolution had disrupted cottage industries and income opportunities for artisans. Automation in fabric making and clothing manufacturing put small weavers out of business. Many German farmers did not own their own land; instead, they grew food for the aristocracy for small or nonexistent wages, and they experienced winter food shortages.

As in Great Britain, displaced German farmers and craftsmen migrated to the cities, hoping to find work. But they were part of a mass exodus from the country, and there were not enough jobs in the cities to go around. Former farmers often found themselves out of work and even worse off than they had been in the country.

To make matters even worse, there was limited freedom of political thought in Germany in the early 1800s. The government gave little quarter to dissension; even student movements could be outlawed. These strictures extended to religious thought.

German writer and utopian Gottfried Duden has often been blamed for selling poverty-stricken Germans a fantasy of what life would be like in the New World. Duden was something of a social philosopher. He was disturbed by the poverty, crowding, and overpopulation of his fatherland. So, when he traveled to the United States, it was with an eye to where Germans might relocate and enjoy a quality of life that had become impossible in Germany itself.

He traveled to North America's Midwest in 1824 and settled for three years, during which time he wrote his long-titled manifesto *Bericht über eine Reise nach den westlichen Staaten Nordamerikas und einen mehrjährigen Aufenthalt am Missouri in den Jahren 1824 bis 1827*. This book reports what Duden saw and experienced in the North American Midwest. His praise focuses on the Missouri River Valley between St. Louis and Hermann, Missouri, a stretch of land that takes a little over an hour to traverse by car.

Duden himself was a wealthy man who traveled with a personal farmer and cook. His own experience of Missouri was glorious. He commissioned a house to be built about fifty miles outside of St. Louis. He spent his days duck hunting with Daniel Boone's son, sightseeing, touring lead mines, and exploring the wonders of the natural world in which Missouri is still quite rich.

During the years he spent in Missouri, that state enjoyed unusually mild weather, a respite from the usual freezing winters and frequent summer heat waves. There is no reason to think that he was insincere when he reported to his fellow Germans back home that Missouri was the promised land, a land with a fertile valley, ripe for farming. The Missouri River Valley was much like the Rhineland back home, he wrote, just as beautiful, with just as much potential. Here, Germans could own land, they could work for themselves as farmers, they could live with the dignity that was eluding them in their German lives. The reality that immigrants discovered fell short of the dream that Duden sold, but it must be allowed that some of the immigrants were so desperate that Missouri was and still would be an acceptable risk. It should be noted that Duden was not the only one selling a dream of the New World to struggling Germans. The Giessen Emigration Society also promoted immigration to Missouri as the solution to poverty and a lack of political and religious freedom in Germany.

The Giessen Emigration Society founders were Friedrich Münch, a Lutheran minister; his brother, George; and their brother-in-law Paul Follen. Follen was a lawyer and had been a student at the University of Giessen at the same time as Friedrich. The friends were unabashed utopianists and former student activists; they dreamt of forming an independent German state within the United States. There, in Missouri, they and their followers would correct the mistakes that were confounding the fatherland, and the new German state of Missouri would become a role model for Germans back home.

With this ambitious goal in mind, they led five hundred Germans to the new Rhineland in 1834. The immigrants made camp near the farm and home of Duden, who had, by now, returned to Germany. The Münch brothers built a wine cellar from local wood and limestone in 1881, and that cellar, where wines are still aged, exists today. Today, Mount Pleasant Winery claims the Münch brothers as its founders. The brothers were so successful at making wine that they shipped it all the way to Chicago. According to Paul Roberts, they grew Cynthiana/Norton grapes and made wine from them.[20]

Historians have marked the Giessen emigration a failure, although it is hard to mark it as a worse disaster than the voyage of the Mayflower and the early settlement of New England. Quite a few members of the Giessen expedition came down with cholera. In general, they lacked the survival skills needed to pioneer what was effectively a wilderness frontier. Disappointed with the reality of life in Missouri, some members returned to Germany, and there were a number of suicides.

But others survived, recruited Germans back home to join them, despite the hardships, succeeded at farming, and became part of the abolitionist movement. To their credit, Friedrich Münch and Follen would stay the course of their utopian dream. Where other German immigrants became disillusioned, Friedrich never lost his zeal for an independent life, beholden to no one. In grape growing and winemaking, he found the inner peace and spiritual satisfaction that had eluded him in Germany. The work of a vineyard owner was akin to a religious vocation for him. In one of his books, he writes, "The vinedresser, lord of his own possessions, in daily intercourse with peaceful nature, is a happier and more contented man than thousands of those who, in our large cities, driven about by the thronging crowd, rarely attain true peace and serenity of mind."[21]

Wine grapes, for Friedrich, were nothing less than the medium that elevated people above their scrappy animal nature and paved the way for civilization: "With the growth of the grape every nation elevates itself to a higher grade of civilization—brutality must vanish, and human nature progresses."[22]

Friedrich became a state senator; he lived out the rest of his life and died in Missouri, at the age of eighty-four. Legend has it that he died amid his grapevines, with pruning shears in hand. In 1980, when the United States got around to handing out appellations, the Augusta, Missouri, region, where Mount Pleasant is located, was the first region to be so recognized with an American Viticultural Appellation. Augusta, very near Hermann, was so recognized in part because of the influence of glaciers on the soil.

The German Settlement Society of Philadelphia brought the next major influx of Germans to Missouri. Their unlikely leader, George Bayer, was an organist and music teacher who had immigrated to Philadelphia from Baden, Germany. Bayer purchased 11,300 Missouri acres, west of St. Louis, for $1.38 an acre. This would become the wine-producing hub known as Hermann, Missouri.

Like the Giessen group, the German Settlement Society of Philadelphia believed in German superiority to all other ethnic groups and wished to establish an undiluted German community, free of the evils of assimilation. Even the English language was something that should be eschewed, if possible, the emigrants believed. (It must be noted that Hermann's German descendants today speak fluent English.)

They were also well-educated secularists, tolerant of religion, but much more interested in literature, music, and the performing arts. They were not above enjoying a good block party. Wine scholar Thomas Pinney notes that the Hermannites built a theater before they bothered with a church.[23] These highly literate grape farmers became known, regionally, as the "Latin peasants," a nickname that poked fun at their education while also honoring it.

These German immigrants had also read Duden's work or were at least familiar with its ideas. They arrived in Missouri expecting to see the fabulous landscapes and unlimited opportunities that Duden had described. Immediately, however, they found quite a few flies in the utopian ointment. Durden had, in their opinion, not given sufficient warning about how little welcome European settlers could expect from the native Americans. The mild weather of Durden's stay turned out to be an anomaly. The immigrants arrived in the middle of winter. The cold was brutal; summers often scorching. Most importantly, the land was much stonier and less arable than what they had been led to believe. The giant grapevines were as Duden had advertised, but the new settlers quickly learned that grapes were the only crop they could raise on this soil. A further problem was that many of these immigrants had no farming experience. They had been artisans, poets, and philosophers, not growers. The dream of free land and land ownership quickly gave way to the worry about what exactly they were going to do with this free land.

Luckily, there was and always will be, world without end, a healthy and timeless demand for wine. Along with death and a flexible moral code, wine drinking binds humanity and reminds us that we are, after all, one species. So, the German settlers in Hermann threw their legendary German work ethic and efficiency at winemaking.

Like so many American farmers, they first tried to grow European wine grapes. And, as had all experiments up to that point, this effort failed. Then they discovered that wine could be made from the native Catawba and Isabella grapes, both subspecies of *Vitis labrusca*. A Cincinnati man named Nicholas Longworth had developed a method for mollifying the foxiness of the Catawba. At tremendous expense, which involved recruiting

Champagne makers from France, Longworth had learned how to make a sparkling Catawba wine, which involved, among other things, a longer fermentation period. Proving that much wine lore is pure snobbery, this sparkling concoction made its way overseas, where it was compared to and sometimes preferred to French Champagne itself.

Using Longworth's methods, the Missouri Germans succeeded, where others had failed, in making a drinkable wine from wild grapes. Though foxy, this wine could be taken to market, and it quickly found customers among wine-starved midwesterners who were, by that time, none too picky about their refreshing adult beverage as long as some was to be had.

Mistakes were made as the Germans transitioned from amateur to professional winemakers. They did not initially realize how quickly barrels could be contaminated or how easily wine spoils. Their first wine storage facilities were suboptimal. Eventually, they would learn to measure the sugar in the grapes before processing. They learned from their mistakes and soon triumphed in this brand-new venture.

Relative to utopian social experiments in general, Hermann succeeded quite rapidly. Kliman notes that the immigrants' lack of actual winemaking experience worked to their advantage because they "were not beholden to long-held notions of what constituted a proper wine."[24] So what if the wine were foxy and sweet, as long as people bought it, then came back and bought some more?

The Hermann settlement was started up by a mere nine adults and eight children. One really has no choice but to wonder at their bravery. But more settlers joined them, and ten years from the settlement's founding, there were twenty-eight grape growers in their community. These farmers produced 584 gallons of wine.[25] The next year, that amount nearly doubled. It was cause for a public celebration in which they shot off a cannon in honor of Bacchus, the Roman wine god.[26]

But how does all of this relate to Cynthiana, the wine I'm chasing? Have patience; it circles back around. Though they succeeded rather beautifully with the *Vitis labrusca* grapes, where others had failed, the Hermann winemakers remained on the lookout for better grapes. In 1846, a Norton vine made its way to Hermann from Cincinnati, Ohio, and fell into the hands of one Jacob Rommel, who had been a baker back in Germany. Rommel grew this grape and made wine. This was a fortunate chain of events because the Catawba grape on which the colony had come to rely fell victim to disease and declined in productivity. Today, over 170 years later, Hermann's claim to fame is its Norton/Cynthiana wine.

The Norton grape initially looked unimpressive to the Hermannites who, by now, were used to working with the big, bright Catawba. This new grape was smaller and a dull, almost black purple. But it produced a decent wine and, most importantly, did not wither on the vine or succumb to rot or mildew as did the Catawba.

At this point, the heroic story of Missouri wine moves to the personage of George Husmann, who appointed himself the task of becoming an expert on all things wine grape. He was a child in 1838 when his family moved from Hanover, Germany, to Hermann. Husmann's childhood was a mixture of homely tasks, such as driving oxen, selling cheese at the market, and learning English and French as well as the intricacies of German literature from his well-read older brother Fritz.

Such a childhood might seem idyllic, but it was short lived. By the age of twenty, Husmann was an orphan, his beloved brother had died of typhoid, and one of his sisters had moved away from Hermann. He would have been bereft but for a remaining sister who had married into one of Missouri's fruit and winemaking families, the Teubners.

These successful farmers had eight hundred vines and fruit trees on their estate. When Husmann moved in with his sister and her husband, it was a matter of course that he would apprentice as a winemaker. Husmann had that rare talent for loving exactly what you have been given. Grapes became his passion. He reveled in their beauty and anatomy as if they were the Elgin Marbles or the Eiffel Tower. They were endlessly fascinating; a lifetime spent learning about them would be too short.

He devoured books on horticulture, reading well into the night and burning lamp oil. He taught himself the vine growers' techniques for layering and grafting. When his brother-in-law and sister died in rapid succession, the young Husmann inherited their farm. He was a capable farmer, but his legacy is wine scholarship and advocacy.

Husmann's main contribution to the fledgling Missouri wine industry was to champion it along in the face of some damning criticism from Ohio's Nicholas Longworth, then considered the father of American wine, and his partner, John Zimmerman.

Zimmerman told the Hermannites that they should just sell grape juice because, in his opinion, they knew nothing about winemaking. Then Longworth pronounced the Norton grape to be "worthless" for wine. This double whammy from the wine gods demoralized Hermann's growers and winemakers. Many abandoned the wine industry. Husmann did not. He rallied the Norton growers, and these loyalists kept wine culture alive in Hermann. In 1855, Husmann introduced the Concord grape into the Hermann winegrowing mix. By 1859, he had built his own Missouri winery.

Hermann's wine industry took a bad blow from the Civil War, but not for lack of patriotism. Husmann enlisted on the side of the Union. Most, if not all, of the Hermannites were antislavery, and Husmann was no exception. According to Kliman, Husmann was a member of the Missouri Radical Republicans, who met with Abraham Lincoln in person to ask him to emancipate slaves.[27]

His military career lasted less than two years, but during that time, Hermann's vines were neglected. Confederate soldiers camped out on Husmann's own vineyard, destroying the crop and necking back all his wine and cider. They did $10,000 worth of damage, but Husmann and Hermann survived the war and continued to make wine.

In a delightful twist of irony, Nicholas Longworth came around on the subject of the Norton grape and wine. Before he died in 1863, he wrote to Husmann asking for a Norton cutting. Longworth's son-in-law, who also became his winery manager, published a book in which he put both hope and faith in Norton's Virginia Seedling.

In 1866, Husmann shot back at any remaining Norton critics with the publication of his book, *Cultivation of the Native Grape*. This book was widely respected, and Husmann positioned himself as a rival American wine father, competing with the late Longworth for that title. This and the success of his farm and others who grew and processed Norton boosted Hermann's wine industry. Ohio, the presumed seat of American wine, had a challenger.

After saving Missouri's wine industry from the ravages of Longworth, Zimmerman, and a civil war, Husmann became a professor of forestry and pomology at the University of Missouri. Then he relocated to California, where he was among the pioneers of wine culture in Napa Valley.

In his middle age, Husmann made an about-face that seems to some wine historians like a terrible betrayal. He relegates the Norton grape to medicinal uses in the *Missouri Yearbook of Agriculture* and then adds these damning words: "The Norton is no market grape at all."[28] He does not even pause in his discourse to explain what he means by that, instead moving right along to a discussion of improper fruit handling. Kliman likens this betrayal to leaving a loyal wife of many years for a young, exciting mistress. Missouri had built a national wine industry around the Norton and the native Concord. Missouri wines had been imported everywhere. Virginia Norton had won prizes all over Europe.

The elevation of Norton wine to the status of world champion has a lot to do with a Hermannite named Michael Poeschel. According to Kliman, Poeschel started "from nothing and with nothing."[29] He was a wool spinner in Altenburg, Saxony, who arrived in Hermann in 1839, knowing nothing of farming, grapes, or winemaking.

Yet he was one of those men who will succeed at anything he sets his mind to. He was hardworking and perceptive, with an as-yet-untested knack for business. Surely, those Germans who immigrated to the hard winters of Missouri must have felt some frustrated greatness within themselves. Why else take so massive a risk? Maybe they didn't know yet how that greatness would manifest, but they knew it needed more space, more breathing room, cheap land, and a certain freedom from the shackles of tradition and expectation.

Just as the bumblebee flies in blissful ignorance of the mechanics of flying, Poeschel had so little experience with wine, he didn't know the failure rate of such an enterprise. No less a personage than Thomas Jefferson had striven for years to make a decent wine with American agricultural products. Yet with all the resources at his disposal, he failed even in his own estimation.

According to Pinney, Poeschel produced his first bottle of Hermann wine in 1846, using the grape of the Isabella vine, a grape grown by Jacob Fugger.[30] Isabella is a close relative of the sweet and juicy Concord grape and one of the many hybrids of *Vitis vinifera*, the European grape stock, and America's native *Vitis labrusca*. Many people agree that the Isabella grape is not wine worthy.

Poeschel soon began growing his own grapes, and his earliest wines also included the foxy Catawba. Colonials had mostly pronounced the native grapes as miserable ingredients with which to make undrinkable wine. Once again, we see the importance of the winemaker in producing something people will actually buy. Where others had seen only trash, Poeschel saw a viable ingredient and created a marketable product.

Poeschel's early success with the *labrusca*-based wines was modest but startling, considering that he had, starting out, only seven-eighths of an acre on which to grow. He used some kind of trellis to grow the fruit in flat sheets. He was an early practitioner of intensive gardening practices. And we can deduce that he walked, inspected, and groomed his vines several times a week. One visitor to his acre wrote of seeing a "wall of grapes and . . . not a single rotten berry."[31]

Poeschel sold batches of wines locally and regionally. In 1848, a group of Weinfest partiers, in a town where almost everyone made wine, traveled the twenty miles to Poeschel's winery to continue the party. Clearly, his two-year-old *labrusca* hybrids had distinguished themselves in some way.

The next year, Poeschel wrote, in German, to a St. Louis newspaper, the *Western Journal*, in response to an information request from that periodical. In that letter, he reveals that he had already committed his resources entirely to the Catawba grape. It was the only grape that would grow in that area that made good wine. It is worth noting that he qualifies this declaration with the words "as far as our experience tells us."[32] In his letter to the newspaper, Poeschel admits to making $1,600 in a recent year from his grapes and another $400 from wood. The amount he made from grapes had more than doubled year over year.

The sale of wood is something of a puzzle until we remember that most of those Missouri households would have gotten through the winters with wood-burning stoves. Grapevines have fallen out of favor as heating fuel, but these German immigrants would be loath to waste any resource. And the grapevine conveys a particular taste to certain foods, so it has special utility as a cooking fuel. Poeschel was a savvy businessman; grapevines have to be cut back to be maximally productive, so it made sense to market them as fuel. And selling off unproductive first-year vines and suckers would offer a steady sideline to balance the higher risks of grape growing.

By all accounts, Poeschel was a modest, grounded man who made no claims to greatness for himself. However, when it came to the Hermann wine-growing community, he was an enthusiastic booster. "I think the world will be our market after a short while," he says in that same letter to St. Louis readers, adding, "We will strive to diminish importation of foreign wines. The grape has never failed here, as long as this settlement exists."[33]

Poeschel's superior success in winemaking, when he was growing and pressing the same grapes as everyone else in Hermann, is something of an unsolved mystery. His process was an open book; he was happy for anyone to read how he made his wines and discloses his methods in that same letter. But there are indications of meticulousness in his descriptions. He washed his harvested grapes and let them dry for a specific amount of time, he reveals. About rot, he writes, "The rot . . . is very trifling and imperceptible among the abundance of grapes which remain."[34] Well. That may have been an understatement. Any grape grower has to guard against rot, and today's growers avail themselves of a host of antifungal chemicals, unless they have committed to organic growing. Poeschel would not have had access to those sprays.

Guarding against grape rot in the 1800s was a matter of removing affected grapes and leaves, quickly, because rot spreads very fast. Affected grapes and leaves cannot simply be thrown on the ground because they will spread rot back up the vines, possibly quicker than if the offending vegetation had not been removed. Preventing rot also involves regulating the flow of water to keep it from spreading fungus from one cluster or vine to another and ensuring equitable airflow, even in very tightly grown vine rows.

We can be reasonably sure that Hermann growers had to manually towel dry their grapes quite frequently. Poeschel writes about how he made wine, and in that description, we find nothing unique; he may have considered the prosaic work of grooming his grapes unworthy of discussion. What grower would not protect his fruit? However, that near-perfect "wall of grapes" that one visitor noticed had to be the result of some very careful cultivation.

The *Western Journal* appears to have published Poeschel's letter in its entirety. Though exceedingly modest, no word in it was irrelevant. The editors even left in this touching admission: "Cheerfully would I and my neighbors subscribe for your periodical, but we don't understand the English language."[35]

By 1858, Norton's Virginia Seedling had made its way to Hermann, via the Prince horticulturists who sent a sample to Husmann. Poeschel was not a man to miss an opportunity. So by the time he expanded his business and took on a partner, he was making both Norton and Cynthiana wines as well as wines from grapes already well established in Hermann. According to Kliman, Poeschel believed that the Cynthiana grape had its origins in Arkansas.

Part of Poeschel's business savvy was knowing when to expand, not hazarding his success by outgrowing his resources, that mistake having ruined many an enterprise. So he was a ripe, but not old, fifty-two when he recruited a partner, one John Scherer, a fellow German immigrant living in Detroit. By this time, Poeschel was married with children.

Scherer and Poeschel built a solid two-story winery that stands today. This would be the winery's administrative center. Poeschel and his family made their living quarters upstairs. Smaller buildings were erected for pressing, bottling, and barreling.

The buildings were sturdy but nondescript. Scherer and Poeschel put their inventive genius into their winemaking equipment. They had a winepress that crushed the grapes between large wooden rollers and piped the juice directly into barrels through holes cut into the floor separating the press room from the cellar.

Kliman notes that the "brute efficiency" of the Poeschel and Scherer enterprise allowed them to make wines of "uncommon grace and depth."[36] By May 1871, Husmann's monthly *Grape Culturist* showed how well the two winemakers had diversified their grapes and wines. That periodical acknowledges several vintages from Poeschel and Scherer, including a white Traminer, from a Delaware vine; an Iona; a Taylor; a Catawba; and a white Concord. These vintages all earned a "best," "excellent," or "one of the best" from the *Grape Culturist*'s reviewers.[37]

Poeschel and Scherer came to dominate wine culture in Hermann, and the company changed its name to Stone Hill in 1883.[38] And by that name, the wine enterprise still exists. But before that name change, Poeschel and Scherer racked up some rich and strange accolades. "Rich," because these were really solid international awards, judged by formidably accredited field experts. "Strange," because the Norton was a new grape, and the very new Norton wine could not have reasonably expected to outsoar European vintages that had been cultivated for centuries. And yet it did.

Oh, to have been alive in 1873 and attended the Vienna World's Fair. To have seen the Rotunda before it burned down. For almost a hundred years, it boasted the largest man-made dome in the world, larger than the Pantheon. There, the inventors, the scholars, the scientists, the connoisseurs, and, yes, the reviewers gathered to celebrate one another's ingenuity. From May to November, well over seven million people would visit and enthuse over the myriad of man's creations. No more positive testament to the human spirit exists than the world's fairs, the brainchild of Britain's Prince Albert, a tireless enthusiast for modern invention and scientific discovery.

To this fair, twenty thousand bottles of wine from many parts of the world traveled to vie for recognition. Europe was well represented. California wines were already in the mix, but one of the judges boldly noted that the wines made from the native Norton and Cynthiana grapes were better than the European wines made in California. Only three American wineries came away from that event with medals of merit, and the Poeschel Norton was one.

The same judge who awarded the Norton declared that Missouri was well placed to be not only the most "prolific" of U.S. wine producers but also the best wine producer. Take that, California. Five years later, the world's fair was held in Paris, and there, too, the Norton took a medal. In 1889, when the fair was again in Paris, the Norton repeated its success near the shadow of the newly constructed Eiffel Tower.

In 1883, when Poeschel sold his winery and vineyard to William Herzog and George Stark, he must have felt that he could rest on some very fine laurels indeed. In time, George passed the business along to his sons, Ottmar and Louis. Under the Starks, the Stone Hill Winery became a huge enterprise; the company continued making wine but diversified into harder liquors, especially fruited brandies, gin, whisky, and bourbon, which was, at that time, the name for any corn-based whisky. Wine became a minority percentage of the spirits made at Stone Hill.

Missouri vineyards and wineries found it difficult to compete with a developed wine industry in California. The endless California growing season made growing grapes there cheaper. And California was able to replicate the familiar European vintages. The known European vintages were a comfort zone for many wine drinkers. Having diversified its product line, Stone Hill was safer than other wineries going into the twentieth century. But it was not safe against Prohibition.

A lesser-known fact about Prohibition is that there was no centralized mechanism for enforcing it. It had to have local support. Rhode Island refused to ratify the Eighteenth Amendment. That state had already voted to enact Prohibition on a state level in the 1800s. The experiment ended after temperance leader Burrill Arnold was murdered. You could say that Rhode Island knew, in advance, how Prohibition would go and refused to go there again.

Voters in Connecticut similarly rejected the federal law and partied hard the day that Prohibition was declared federally. Connecticut would not be the only state where imbibing alcohol would increase during Prohibition. New York ratified the new amendment, in writing, but the collective immigrant community refused its enforcement. Recent immigrants to the United States saw Prohibition as an attack on their moderate-drinking culture, with some justice.

In Maryland, the Eighteenth Amendment was ratified, but the state simultaneously refused to allow enforcement of it. Maryland's governor stood with the state's immigrant population in opposing the amendment throughout its lifespan.

It might be time to make an obvious point: sobriety *is* a healthy option. That said, Prohibition in America had little to do with sobriety and everything to do with racism and profiling. Nothing points to this problem more clearly than the alliance of Prohibitionists with the Ku Klux Klan (KKK). The KKK proudly supported Prohibition, and Prohibition empowered the KKK, which functioned as a terrorist group under the banner of enforcing the new amendment.

"The Klan's main targets were immigrants from southern and eastern Europe, especially Catholic ones. Prohibition advocates had already linked them with drinking and criminality, and for these people, the era was a time of raids, violence, and terror," writes Becky Little of the History Channel.[39] Where states refused ratification of the Eighteenth Amendment or refused to enforce it, they were, to that extent, protecting their recent immigrants.

Prohibition literature also strongly conflated the German enemy with the consumption of alcohol in slogans like "A dry vote is a vote against the Kaiser" and "The Kaiser Must Go! The Saloon Must Go!"[40] This fuzzy thinking was a precursor for the conflation of 9/11 and the drug war.

The emphatic shutdown of winemaking in Hermann could only be accomplished with the compliance of anti-German Missourians. To understand the anti-German sentiment in Missouri, we have to return to the philosophy of the earliest German immigrants. They strongly believed that German culture was superior and should be cherished and maintained in productive exile. The prevailing English-speaking culture should be respected but not emulated. Hermannites had clung hard to their Germanic folkways, even giving Hermann the nickname "Vaterland," meaning "fatherland" in German.

Hermannites had peacefully resisted assimilation, preferring their German language and culture to that of the mainstream. To that end, teachers and children spoke German in school, dozens of German-language publications circulated, church services were conducted in German, and even some government duties and documents were executed in German. Successive generations sustained a German-speaking-only culture about which the Hermannites neither boasted nor apologized.

When viewed from a certain angle, this non-assimilation seemed un-American, unpatriotic, especially to jealous Americans who had not prospered as had so many Hermannites. The wealth and comfort of the Hermannites must have seemed easy to their English-speaking neighbors who had not seen (or had managed to ignore) the hardscrabble start of the first Germans in Missouri. The bare survival of hard winters, the beginnings of a wine industry clawed out of stony ground with unpracticed hands, the trial and error, the disappointments—those years of desperation were behind the winemakers of Hermann. They seemed to have always had their silver spoons.

Stone Hill Winery, in particular, had prospered, becoming the second-largest winery in the country after the Civil War and producing over a million gallons of booze a year.[41] The advent of World War I widened the gulf between these peaceful isolationists and the broader community. Anti-German feeling, stoked by the role of Germany in the war, quickly changed things in St. Louis and beyond. German place-names became anglicized. German churches also anglicized their names and either started conducting services in English or closed their doors on Sundays.

The triumphant celebrations at the end of World War I in 1918 transitioned almost seamlessly into the triumphant destruction of German vineyards and wineries in Missouri in 1919. Perhaps no group stirred up prejudice against the Missouri Germans more than the Missouri Council of Defense, which lobbied to outlaw the use of German across all the state's institutions in language reminiscent of the Nazis. "The Council believes that the elimination of German and the universal use of English . . . is essential to the development of a true, patriotic sentiment among all the people," that group declared.[42]

Stone Hill Winery, under the leadership of Ottmar Stark, must have hoped for an eleventh-hour reprieve, a reprieve such as the immigrants of New York and Maryland had been afforded by their state. Carrie Nation was not there in person to plunge her hatchet into hard-won barrels full of wine and spirits. But on July 1, 1919, under federal orders, Stark reluctantly authorized his own staff to drain the wine barrels, destroy the winemaking equipment, and tear up the vines.

The English speakers of Missouri got their revenge against the Kaiser and the seemingly easy success of the German Americans in one fell swoop. Nothing short of squandered red wine, gushing into the fields as if it had been torn from an enemy's vein, would do.

Stone Hill Winery, that grand old man of midwestern wines, ceased wine production; its wine cellars were converted to growing mushrooms.[43] Other growers converted their grape fields to Concord and grew sweet grapes for jelly and juice. The Welch's company was the largest buyer of this product. Commercial wine production in Hermann was mostly lost for more than forty years. Home winemaking and bootlegging flourished, however, which may have been the salvation of the Norton grape. When the wine industry returned, after Prohibition, California, not Missouri, would dominate the market.

* * *

The U.S. wine industry made a shift to California that seems at first glance to have taken place overnight. It did not take place overnight, of course. Californians had been growing grapes and making wine since 1769. Catholic missionary Padre Junipero Serra planted grapevines and seeds as he was establishing a chain of missions.

Through the early 1870s, however, this wine remained a mostly local product. California winemakers made wine for Californians, and Ohio and Missouri made wine that was exported to the rest of the country. But in 1875, California lawmakers successfully lobbied for a tariff on imported European wines.

This meant that East Coast wineshops found it desirable to stock California wines for mid-price consumers. From Europe, they imported the more high-end wines; there would always be just enough wealthy wine purchasers to make it worth paying the tariff on the expensive products.[44] Americans now had much less exposure to Europe's mediocre wines, and we would, over time, conclude that European wines were overall better, even though they are not.

Another factor in the decline of Missouri's wine industry was urbanization. Farming is hard, and it was even harder before the advent of highly mechanized farming. Given an opportunity, young people would often leap to jobs in the cities, which paid better and were not at the mercy of the weather and inconsistent harvests. Life in the cities, including urban amenities, like electricity and running water, may have seemed easier to the children raised on Missouri's farms in the early 1900s.

Yet another change swept in to give California dominance over America's wine culture: the railroad. The transcontinental, completed in 1869, made it possible to export California wine to all parts of the United States quickly and affordably.

Fast-forward over 150 years into the future. I walk into a Kentucky wine store. There's an interesting collection. I ask the owner, who is also manning the register, whether he has any local or regional wines. No, he says. People won't drink it. It's no good. Not even Huber? I ask him, invoking the one local vineyard that's widely known in these parts. It's crap, he avers (not in those exact words). If people won't buy it, he can't stock it. Of American-made wines, only California wines are worth drinking and stocking, he explained to me.

This conversation gets repeated in wineshops all over the midwestern United States and other parts of the country, in different accents and with different words. But the message is the same: in the United States, only California makes decent wine.

Let's break that down, shall we? California was the first state in the United States where the old European vines, all of them based on *Vitis vinifera*, could grow. And, oh boy, do they grow in California. With twelve months of summer, California can grow grapes in its sleep. And, until the high cost of land and insurance caught up with it, those grapes could be grown on the cheap.

Early California viniculture got a huge boost from all those panhandlers who did not strike gold, were stranded in California, and now needed jobs. How many gold panners who didn't get rich had to settle for pruning vines in the hot, desert-like California heat? Hard to quantify.

California can grow grapes year-round. The state effectively has no winter. So the price of grapes grown in California dropped. That lowered the price of grapes for all grape growers, including growers in Missouri and Ohio, where growing grapes for one season was hard work and costly. California got the ascendancy in the U.S. wine industry for one reason and one reason only: California could do it cheaper. Not better. Cheaper.

Kliman has noted that the Hermann wine industry—so carefully cultivated over thirty years, so hard won by righteous, enterprising immigrants who arrived in the wilderness with nothing but their ingenuity—had already taken a bad hit from cheap and easy California grapes before Prohibition.

Picture me whacking my ear here. Really? California wine was just cheaper? But . . . Prohibition, right? Prohibition killed the U.S. wine industry, and California saved it, right? This is how California saved the wine industry. It quickly pivoted to making grape juice. The Eighteenth Amendment did not, contrary to popular thinking, outlaw the consumption of alcoholic beverages; it outlawed the commercial production of them. Householders could drink wine, and it was legal to make your own wine at home. So anyone who wanted wine with dinner imported grapes—or even just juice—from California and fermented their own wine. (I guess this is as good a time as any to mention that you can make wine out of Welch's frozen grape juice concentrate. Add yeast and pectin. Put it all in a sealed barrel. Wait two days. If you are not particular, you now have wine. If you are desperate, you also have wine.)

California grape growers made a killing during Prohibition. The cost of grape juice rose; where there had been a gold rush, there was now a rush to grow grapes. And you didn't have to know how to make wine. Amateurs welcome.

Here's another ear slapper: some California farmers lost money after Prohibition ended because they had torn up their lovely wine grapes and planted more hardy grapes that could make the journey to New York without being reduced to mush. *Vitis vinifera* would have to be replanted. But that was okay because of the twelve-month summer.

3

Where's the Wine in My Old Kentucky Home?

Kentucky has bourbon. Kentucky has horses. You know all this. What you might not know is that Kentucky is still experiencing negative impacts from Prohibition. That is why I decided to look at Prohibition and the return of the wine industry from the point of view of Kentucky. To my amazement, the Norton grape has a considerable part to play in this renaissance. Several of the vineyards I visited in my home state were growing and making Norton wines.

Kentucky became my home state in 2013, when I became very ill with a hereditary kidney and liver condition. Working full-time became difficult and problematic because of all the time I had to spend in hospitals and waiting rooms. I fell back on freelance writing, and my husband, Joel, and I moved to Louisville, Kentucky, where the cost of living was more in proportion to my small income. In Kentucky, I could afford to be sick and still own a house, a shared car, a dog, and four cats. In a pinch, we could have lived on Joel's income, but my odd freelance writing and editing jobs made a decent contribution to our lifestyle.

Somewhere in all this, I fell in love with Kentucky in general, and Louisville in particular. This is not to say that Louisville does not have serious problems. It does, and the killing of innocent Black civilians Breonna Taylor and David McAtee points to a terrible underlying racism that plays out in the city's east-west divide. While millennial homebuyers stage bidding wars on houses selling for $250,000 on the city's east side, west-side sellers struggle to unload their two-bedroom, one-bath houses for more than $50,000.

Then there's the deforestation. Louisville has been so cavalier about chopping trees and so slow and lazy about replanting that our summer temperatures are consistently higher than those in Nashville, a two-hour drive to the south. In related news, our air is tragically bad, not always in the red zone, but often enough that we might as well be living on a Chicago freeway.

But I fell in love with Louisville, with the Victorian district and its turreted redbrick mansions, with the shotgun houses, the rows of structurally identical and yet each highly individualized little houses, all doors and windows. In spring, fall, and summer, people sit outdoors at restaurants and coffee shops like they do in Paris and Manhattan. And most Kentuckians are basically kind. In Kentucky, I have made friends who like me for who I am and not what I can do for them. But mostly what I love is that Kentucky is an underdog. It has emerged from extreme poverty, miserable infrastructure, prejudice, mountaintop destruction, black lung, and opioid addiction, and it came out throwing punches. Damaged, but still standing. Like me. Kentucky is such an underdog that, when I tell people I moved here from Georgia, Kentuckians usually ask why.

According to most sources, America's wine industry actually began in my adoptive home state. The history of wine in Kentucky begins with Jean Jacques Dufour, who changed his name to John James as part of his self-reinvention as an American. He was born in 1763 in the Lake Geneva region of Switzerland to a winemaking family. According to his autobiography, Dufour formed a plan to be an American winemaker when he was only fourteen.

He had read that the French soldiers who fought in the Seven Years' War complained bitterly, among other things, of their lack of wine. (Swiss historian Petra Koci quips that "perhaps a sip of good wine might have brought more consensus" to the French and English who were killing each other over territory.)[1]

Dufour, being the wine scholar he was, got out his atlas and checked the latitudes. Yes, there were wine-growing regions all over America that were on the same latitudes as European vineyards. Yet, this New World hungered for decent wine, and making an American wine had, so far, eluded great men, including Thomas Jefferson.

Wine historian Thomas Pinney hypothesizes that, when Dufour studied viticulture in his home country, he did so with the long game in mind: he would be the one to bring wine to America. In 1796, at the age of thirty-three, around the same age that Jesus set out to fulfill his mission, Dufour sailed to America.[2]

It is dangerous to speculate on the motives of historical personages. Dufour was the eldest of many siblings. He might have wished to unburden his family of his support just as much as he wished to enact a great destiny. To the other ship passengers, he might not have made a charismatic impression. He was significantly disabled, having a right arm that ended at the elbow. Furthermore, he was not a wealthy man; he booked passage in steerage.

Yet, when he arrived in America, he brought fifteen years of experience working with his winemaking father. The young Dufour did his homework in the New World. He surveyed the vineyards in Pennsylvania and New York, observing, "So far, I've seen only discouraging attempts at viticulture here in the East. Now I'm curious to know if there is more potential further west."[3] He visited various possible sites for his future vineyard and studied Pierre Legaux, who had enjoyed a modicum of success as a grape grower. To research what had already been accomplished in American winemaking was to mostly study a series of mistakes, many of them lamentably redundant.

At that time in American history, Lexington, Kentucky, was the westernmost outpost of true civilization. It had enough residents and successful businesses to support winemaking, yet it was untrammeled by previous vineyard failures. The weather was just good enough to support grape growing. There were fewer sunny days overall in central Kentucky than there were in New York, but there was an equal amount of rain.

The year 1796 found Dufour on horseback, exploring the banks of the Kentucky River. Nearness to a river was imperative, as he planned to make wine for a nation, not just a region. And that wine would need to be loaded onto big boats and transported to all the main urban hubs. It was also important to find a plot of good farmland. Such a plot presented itself near the juncture of Hickman Creek and the Kentucky, where both waterways dropped a fortune of rich soil, heavy in alluvium.

In 2022, Wine Enthusiast reported that "while there's no such thing as perfect soil, some winemakers believe alluvial soils are as good as it gets."[4] By 1799, Dufour had purchased 750 acres of this desirable farmland. To raise the capital for his enterprise, Dufour established and sold stock in the

Kentucky Vineyard Society. According to the *Kentucky Gazette*, where Dufour advertised his new venture, shares were fifty dollars each, and Kentuckians were nothing if not eager to drink a decent wine.

In the gazette, Dufour bravely announced that he would be producing Kentucky wine, to be relished right in Kentucky, within four years. Kentucky was, at that time, already producing bourbon whiskey. But this new vineyard would produce something more elegant, something that ladies could sip out of crystal glasses at a formal dinner.

Dufour's enterprise attracted the attention and support of John Bradford, an influential editor working at the gazette. The legendary lawyer Henry Clay, then a young man, was an early subscriber to Dufour's Kentucky Vineyard Society. Dufour raised $10,000 and bought 633 acres on the Kentucky River, between Lexington and Louisville. He also bought five slave families, a fact that would dismay his Swiss relatives when they arrived later.[5] His new acres would be the home of First Vineyard. Dufour believed he was well on his way to being America's most legendary winemaker. His plan hit a snag, however, when a naval war foiled his attempt to return to Europe for the grapevines he intended to grow.

Dufour was getting ready to make the same mistake that other aspiring winemakers would eventually prove futile: he was going to import and grow *Vitis vinifera* from Europe. His inability to book passage from New York may well have saved his enterprise, because it forced him to fall back on grapes that were already growing in North America. Dufour handpicked vines and fruit trees from New York and Maryland. From Spring Mill, North Carolina, he brought Catawba grapes for $388, believing them to be a European vintage.[6] From Spring Mill, he also bought grapes that he believed to be the basis of the African wine Constantia. These turned out to be Alexander grapes, another variation on *Vitis labrusca*.[7]

Despite his careful selection of plants, Dufour had purchased quite a few mostly native grapes out of which he believed he would be making Madeira and Burgundy. He personally escorted these precious vines, via wagon and then boat, back to Kentucky.

Dufour's first two years gave reason for hope. The vines flourished, and new wine flowed. Dufour might have jumped the mark by inviting his many relatives and a few friends to join him in the New World. Seventeen of them had immigrated to Kentucky to join him by the year 1801. But in their third year, the new vines at First Vineyard showed signs of all-out failure, possibly caused by black rot. Dufour had also not predicted the ravages that Kentucky birds would cause when they descended on his crops in flocks.

Francois Michaux, a French botanist, heard of the Dufour vineyard from people in Lexington who were still excited about the Swiss winemaker's bold experiment. He headed to the vineyard in trepidation. Would this Swiss immigrant really take a chunk out of French wine imports to America? By the time Michaux arrived, it was obvious that Dufour would not be making wholly French wine any time soon. Mature grapes were rotting on the ground, and the vines were mostly bare, except for some very poor quality grapes.[8]

But two grapes continued to flourish. One of these was the Cape of Good Hope grape, which, according to Clark, was bred by James Alexander, the gardener for William Penn. It was definitely a grape native to the United States, one that American winemakers are still cultivating. The other grape that succeeded was Bland's Madeira, which may or may not have been related to *Vitis aestivalis*. Dufour made the wise decision to dispense with the failed grape varietals and concentrate on making wine from these two.

In 1803, Dufour's twenty-year-old brother traveled by horseback to the White House to present Thomas Jefferson, then president of the United States, with ten gallons of wine from First Vineyard. "The young wine has promise, but it needs to age more," Jefferson pronounced, tactfully.[9] Evidence has emerged that the proffered wine had been spoiled in transit or production.

Henry Clay, newly elected to the U.S. Senate, was at the same dinner party where Jefferson served that young wine, and he was mortified by the response that the Kentucky wine received. The other diners pulled faces and remarked upon its vile taste. Clay was invested in Dufour's business, however, and he took measures to redeem the reputation of Kentucky wine, sending a bottle of the Dufour Madeira to James Madison.[10] The letter accompanying the bottle referenced the failure of the wine at Jefferson's dinner party: "H. Clay had the mortification to have been present some years ago at the exhibition at Mr. Jefferson's table of some Kentucky wine which having been injured in the process of fermentation was of the most wretched quality."[11]

Clay was a solid fan of Kentucky wines and almost certainly Dufour's biggest supporter, saving his friends and relatives. At a banquet of the Kentucky Vineyard Society, Clay got buzzed enough on the First Vineyard product to raise a glass in praise of both Kentucky wine and the Swiss immigrants who had brought it to America.

Winemaking is a long, long game, and those who do not come to it with independent wealth must manage the risks some other way. Dufour managed the risks of First Vineyard by starting up Second Vineyard in what we today call Indiana, on the banks of the Ohio River. The majority of his Swiss compatriots ended up at Second Vineyard, which eventually showed more promise than the first attempt. The Dufour compatriots optimistically named this settlement New Switzerland. The vineyard would reach the height of its success in 1820, producing twelve thousand gallons of wine.[12]

In 1804, the Kentucky Vineyard Society was deeply in debt, and it was disbanded. Expenses had far outstripped income at First Vineyard. Dufour himself returned to Europe in 1806, ostensibly to pay down debt, but perhaps also to see the wife who had stayed behind in Switzerland. Whether he got caught up in marital bliss or in the chaos of Napoleon's regime, he did not return to America for ten years. He weathered the War of 1812 in his fatherland. But Second Vineyard thrived, even in Dufour's absence. A local resident, who fancied himself something of a scholar and poet, dubbed the Second Vineyard the "Empire of Bacchus." One thing had obviously been missing from midwestern civilization, and that was wine. *Labrusca* had come into its own and earned this praise: "Columbia rejoice! smiling Bacchus has heard / Your prayers of so fervent a tone."[13]

By the time Dufour returned to Kentucky, First Vineyard had been declared an interesting but failed experiment. The Dufour brothers, wives, and children had all moved to Second Vineyard, near which John James built a house and lived for the rest of his life. In 1826, he published *The Vinedresser's Guide*, a book that was, for a time, the definitive text on grape growing in America. In that book, Dufour repeated the oft-sounded plea for native wines and an industry that would liberate the pristine New World from a corrupting dependency on old, evil, undemocratic Europe.

He continued to make wine, and it would be lovely to report that this man of exceptional vision died fully satisfied with his experiment. Unfortunately, he did not. As late as 1819, only eight years before his death, he wrote a letter stating that the Cape and Bland's Madeira grapes, on which he had built his business and his community, never really ripened properly in New Switzerland. We must hope that, upon his death in 1827, he took comfort in knowing that he had at least advanced the knowledge of winemaking by several major leaps.

New Switzerland became a teaching vineyard where knowledge of viticulture was freely shared with other aspiring winemakers. The settlement gave no-cost cuttings to those who asked. But the vineyard declined in the late 1820s, mostly as a result of the economic panics of 1819 and 1825. Pinney also blames rot, disease, and pests for ending the Vevay vineyards. (Some nights, the Vevay grape growers had to spend hours ridding their rows of cricket infestations; it was, indeed, a strange new world with small, bizarre monsters.) He also notes that the unenthusiastic second generation was less committed to fighting for wine.[14] Today, all that is left of Second Vineyard is the Swiss Wine Festival, which the Indiana town of Vevay celebrates annually in August. That and a two-hundred-year-old barrel, smashed in on one side, which a local family owns and maintains as a curio. According to Swiss historian Petra Koci, no grapevines grow in Vevay. The town's one winemaker gets his grapes and juices from elsewhere.

That was not the end of wine in Kentucky, however. In 1814, John Francis Buchetti was making wine in the unprepossessingly named Barren County, Kentucky. He had been a teacher in Vevay who struck out on his own to try his winemaking fortunes. Like all American winemakers, he was on a quest to find or cultivate or hybridize a better grape.

A letter to winemakers in Indiana shows him growing the standard Cape, the Madeira, and a little-known white varietal called Chassloss, which was first cultivated in Switzerland. In that same letter, he begs the Indiana winemakers to send him a slip of a vine they think has promise.[15] James Hicks lived near Buchetti and also grew grapes and made wine. Colonel James Taylor made wine, possibly only for personal use, in Newport, Kentucky, which he founded. His vines grew on the Ohio River near Cincinnati.

Northern Kentucky came alive with grapevines when the previously humble Catawba grape became the star of its own craze. Catawba, also the name of an Indigenous tribe, was nothing but the mostly despised native American *Vitis labrusca,* got up in a cocktail dress like Eliza Doolittle. But the process of converting this grape to a sparkling, Champagne-like wine made it a celebrity in the wine world. Mostly, this craze took place in Cincinnati, but northern Kentucky, which lies along the same Ohio River, got in on the act.

The Catawba craze arguably began when John Adlum, who had served in the Revolutionary War, announced that he had grown a fabulous wine grape called Catawba in Georgetown, Maryland. According to Pinney, Adlum was famous for putting too much sugar in his wine and cooking the grapes at far too high a temperature. Nevertheless, he made the claim that, in having cultivated the Catawba, he had "done [his] country a greater service than [he] should have done, had [he] paid the national debt."[16] Grandiosity? Or was America precisely that thirsty?

Catawba grapes and wine could not have asked for a better promoter than Adlum, who wrote not one but two books praising the grape and his own winemaking processes. But it was the arrival of Nicholas Longworth in Cincinnati, Ohio, that turned Catawba into the queen of wines and also turned the nearby section of the Ohio River into the "Rhineland of America."

Longworth, who left Newark, New Jersey, and moved to Cincinnati in 1804, is an American rags-to-riches story. He studied and practiced law but made his fortune buying cheap Ohio land that quickly rose in value. He also accepted plots of land as payment for his legal services. When he died in 1863, his estate was worth approximately $2 million.

By 1828, then, he was independently wealthy. He could do exactly whatever he wanted, and what he wanted was to fully engage his interest in horticulture. He had been growing grapes, as a hobbyist, since 1813. With his fortune in real estate made, it was time to see if his Midas touch would extend to winemaking. It would, despite several mistakes. As nearly all pioneers of early American wine did, he planted European varietals, and it was decades before he finally gave up on that as a bad plan. But he also studied the work of Dufour and took an interest in the grapes that succeeded in Kentucky and Indiana.

Longworth's first serious vineyard was a field of Alexander grapes, which he sowed in Delhi, Ohio, and placed under the stewardship of a German grower named Amen. He also planted a Catawba vineyard in the Mount Adams neighborhood of Cincinnati. Both these varietals had been cultivated from the native American *labrusca* grape. To these two vineyards, he added seven others.

Longworth already had the novel idea of making white wine out of red grapes, thus producing not just a different product but also a product superior to earlier efforts with the *labrusca* vines. He was able to produce a wine that was light pink by removing—or, more accurately, hiring people to laboriously remove—the rather tough Catawba grape skins before fermentation. It is worth noting that Longworth was only able to achieve this dream with the labor of German immigrants, who were flooding into Ohio and worked for Longworth for as little as a shilling a day plus meals.[17]

Longworth was probably not the first person to suspect Americans of snobbery regarding their own homegrown wine grapes. And he is definitely not the last. He fairly proved that his clientele would give higher ratings to American wine if they thought it hailed from Europe.

To test this theory, he put labels on his Catawba wines that made them look like German brands. Consumers, he found, favored his wine labeled "Ganz Vorzuglicher," which means nothing in German except "Entirely Superior." This must have both exonerated and exasperated Longworth, who remained steadfast in his determination to make an American wine that Americans could take pride in. America had rejected so many European traditions on the grounds that they were either stale or corrupt. Why continue to subsidize the moral dankness of Europe by preferring its wine?

Longworth certainly had the genius to make a good dry table wine, which was, in fact, his humble goal. And he succeeded in that. His flat white-ish Catawba sold through the 1830s, winning a county fair award in 1833. Americans remained thirsty, and the business grew, if not yet in spectacular leaps and bounds. In the early 1840s, Longworth announced that he would buy all grapes grown in the Ohio River Valley.

And this is where Longworth, an Ohioan, becomes relevant to Kentucky. The Ohio River separates Kentucky from Ohio, and the northern Kentucky side of the Ohio was just as good for growing grapes as the Ohio side. German winemakers had independently determined that the soil and weather of northern Kentucky were similar to those of wine-growing regions in France and Spain.

Several Kentucky towns today function as suburbs of Cincinnati; they are less than an hour's drive away from that metropolis, and the soil and weather in those towns are the same as the soil and weather that were driving the Catawba craze. Dennis Walter, the current-day owner of StoneBrook Winery in Camp Springs, Kentucky, says that his great-great-grandfather was one of the many grape growers and winemakers on the Kentucky side of Ohio in the mid-1800s. Some Kentucky farmers grew for Longworth's industry, and others tried their hands at making their own wine.

Abraham Baker built a wine cellar in the 1850s that still stands. Today it is believed to be the oldest wine cellar in the United States. It is currently the home of the Baker-Bird Winery. Baker had planted his grapes on hills that rise from the Ohio River near Augusta, one of Bracken County's biggest towns. In building up his business, Baker enlisted the help of German immigrants trained in vine dressing. These men also supervised the building of the 26-foot-tall and 104-foot-long cellar, constructed from local stone. The walls are 3 feet thick. Other nearby vineyards were owned by Laban Bradford and August Bandel.

When stunning success in the wine game came for Longworth, it did so by accident, much in the way he made his real estate fortune. In 1842, a batch of Catawba wine went through a second, unintended fermentation and produced a sparkling wine. The second fermentation turned out to be the secret to excellence. This sparkling Catawba immediately stood out as the best wine Longworth had made, even though it had been made entirely by accident. So he leaned into the accident and hired French Champagne-making experts to make this wine commercially.

The learning curve was unusually steep. Famously, bottles exploded en masse because early efforts failed to control expansion caused by air bubbles. Pinney reports that, in a single year, Longworth's enterprise lost forty-two thousand bottles out of a batch of fifty thousand.[18]

It was enough of a setback to give even a self-made millionaire a few moments of self-doubt. Should he stay this course, so obviously strewn with boulders? He soldiered on, and his staff eventually mastered the méthode champenoise to the extent that wine stayed in the bottle, and the product became wildly popular, even inspiring a poem by Henry Wadsworth Longfellow. "There grows no vine / By the haunted Rhine, / By Danube or Guadalquivir, / Nor on island or cape / That bears such a grape / As grows by the Beautiful River," he writes.[19] The "Beautiful River" refers to the Ohio.

According to wine writer Nick Fauchald, by 1859, Ohio was the center of winemaking in the United States. Production exceeded 570,000 gallons of wine annually, double what California was producing.[20] But success, if not always pride, often goes before a fall, and in 1860, just as the Ohio River Valley was poised to be the center of the wine universe, Catawba vines started succumbing to the twin demons of the wine industry: black rot and powdery mildew.

Despite the failure of many Catawba plantings, Kentucky continued to thrive as a grape and winemaking state. Bracken County rose as a major player in American wine grape growing pre-Prohibition. Today, Bracken is a fifty-minute drive from Cincinnati, then maybe a long day's journey by horse and cart.

Unfortunately for wine drinkers, Confederate soldiers invaded Bracken County and burned down fifty buildings during the Battle of Augusta. They somehow missed the Baker wine cellar, which was fortunate for the many Bracken County women and children who were hiding in the tunnels underneath it. The Confederates avoided starvation in part because they were able to forage grapes while they plundered.[21]

Bracken County's resilience in the face of war and destruction should be a matter of historical inquiry. Its wine industry not only weathered the Civil War; it positively bounced back. Alcohol is, after all, the industry that weathers nearly every catastrophe. People always want to enliven their spirits with a chemical boost.

By the late 1800s, Kentucky was the third-largest state producer of wine in the United States. Bracken County produced more wine than any other county in the nation in 1870, and its total wine output was half that of the entire nation's wine production.

A dark cloud hangs over this happy portrait of energetic winemaking. And, at some point, I will have to acknowledge that all this entrepreneurial bliss took place largely at the expense of Indigenous Americans: Cherokee, Chickasaw, Shawnee, and Osage who inhabited Kentucky for twelve thousand years before European settlers murdered and displaced them. According to the Kentuckians for the Commonwealth's "Indigenous Lands Acknowledgement," "Indigenous peoples have always lived on the land that is now called Kentucky and continue to live here today."[22]

Decades of schoolchildren have erroneously been taught that the original Americans did not live in Kentucky but only hunted on the Bluegrass plains. That is not the truth. The Ohio River Valley, so attractive to European farmers, was, naturally, just as attractive to hunters and gatherers who also practiced sustainable farming.

The timeline of wine production in Kentucky is intertwined with the history of displacing Kentucky's oldest tribes. By the end of the Revolutionary War, there were seventy-two European settlements in the Lexington, Kentucky, area. Europeans pretended to make peace with treaties, but encroachment on Indian lands continued inexorably.

In 1819, when Jean Jacques Dufour was finally conceding that European wines wouldn't grow in Indiana or Kentucky, the Kentucky Baptist Mission Society opened a school for Indian boys that was clearly meant to reeducate them in European culture. The school was in Scott County at the Great Crossing, a former buffalo migration route.

In the 1830s, while Longworth was building up his Ohio-based wine industry, Indigenous Kentuckians were driven down the Trail of Tears to land in Oklahoma, along with other Americans from east of the Mississippi. Historians quibble over whether this forced journey was an intentional genocide or an accidental genocide. The details of Indigenous displacement are torturous, but the big picture is as tough to wrap one's head around as the Holocaust. I have a brief, bad moment of hoping that, well, there just weren't that many Native Americans to begin with. Didn't they do a good job of limiting their family size? I have to force myself to google "How many Native Americans died from colonization?"

Fifty-six million, according to CNN.[23] Conflicts with the better-armed white man and forced marches took their toll, of course, but 90 percent of the original inhabitants were killed off by the introduction of smallpox, measles, and influenza to their continent. Our diseases were the worst genocide.

So, when I write about the travails of Kentucky, it starts there. Do I have a right, even, to complain about the destruction of our bourbon and wine industries, the federal government's pressure on growers to convert their fields to tobacco? Our opioid epidemic? Our ongoing dependency on thinning seams of coal? The poverty that is still at close to 17 percent, making us the fifth-poorest state in the nation? I leave it to you to decide, and if you choose to close this book and read no further, I respect that decision.

While Kentucky wine and bourbon makers were busy building up a thriving industry that employed thousands of people and promoted the emergence of a middle class, there were forces working against the production of spirits. In the 1840s and 1850s, while Bracken and other Ohio River Valley counties were growing grapes and providing wine to many parts of the United States, the Washington Society, the Women's Christian Temperance Union (WCTU), and the Knights of Temperance were preaching against the Demon Rum.

Kentucky's 1915 gubernatorial election functions as a microcosm of the conflicts and movements that led up to the nationwide prohibition of alcoholic beverages. The election became almost entirely about selling booze, with Harry V. McChesney running as the Prohibition candidate and Augustus Owsley Stanley running on the anti-Prohibition ticket.

Stanley rather famously pointed out the hypocrisy of candidates, known to be drinkers, who won on the Prohibition platform. "They keep full of booze and introduce bills to punish the man who sells it to them," he once said.[24] Stanley won the election by four hundred votes, demonstrating both how divided the state was and also why you need to quit bothering Jesus and get to the polls.

Stanley continued to support the anti-Prohibition forces in Kentucky. But it proved such a divisive issue that lawmaking came to a near standstill while the General Assembly obsessed over it. The Kentucky General Assembly ratified Prohibition on January 14, 1918. Later that year, the assembly separately voted for a state amendment that redundantly prohibited the sale of alcoholic beverages. Stanley agreed to support the amendment in order to end the conflict and get on with the business of running the state.

When I hear people talk about the impossibility of getting rid of the Electoral College, I think of the Eighteenth Amendment. The Eighteenth Amendment prohibited the sale of alcoholic beverages all over the United States. Within a year of becoming law, Prohibition had lost its luster for those Americans who understood its impact on the economy. Those who could not find replacement jobs when Prohibition shut down the distilleries and breweries didn't love it either. It was *not* impossible to get rid of the Eighteenth Amendment. It simply required another amendment to amend it. The Twenty-First Amendment currently stands as the only legislation that undoes the work of a constitutional amendment. Let us hope it is not the last of its kind.

Prohibition was unkind to the German immigrants of Ohio. It was even unkinder to Kentucky. The advocates of teetotaling were convincing, however, and we cannot entirely blame federal law for the effects of turning Kentucky dry. Kentucky's General Assembly was the first state to confirm the amendment by a vote of 94 to 17. However, nationwide Prohibition was immensely popular with Kentuckians. Kentucky voters showed support for the Volstead Act by implementing their own state ban on alcohol.

Prior to that, individual Kentucky counties could vote on whether to be wet or dry. This "local option" had been enacted by Kentucky lawmakers in 1894. By July 1906, thirteen years before nationwide Prohibition, thirty-nine Kentucky counties had gone dry, and only twenty-five counties still harbored saloons. In fact, according to a 1908 article in the *Annals of the American Academy of Political and Social Science,* there were only fifty-some places in the state where one could wet one's whistle with a splash of alcohol.[25] The Kentucky Anti-Saloon League (ASL) was a major player in Kentucky's backlash against its own wine and bourbon industries.

I have to confess to daydreaming through a lot of my high school and college history classes. So I was surprised to learn that the temperance movement did not grow out of the colonists' general tendency toward religious separatism. The Pilgrims arrived in the New World with very little beer and wine—because they drank most of it on the ships during their sixty-six-day voyage.

In the days before water could be treated municipally, it was often unsafe. The fermentation process made liquids safer by killing off the most toxic bacteria. Getting drunk in public was shaming for a Pilgrim and could land you in the stocks, but just drinking some low-wattage beer was par for the course. John Calvin, spiritual father to the Pilgrims, was not a teetotaler either. Good food and wine were some of the few pleasures he encouraged people to enjoy—they were gifts from god, he maintained.

The great Christian poets of England—John Bunyan and John Milton, famous for *Pilgrim's Progress* and *Paradise Lost*—enjoyed a refreshing adult beverage from time to time. John Wesley, the founder of Methodism, preached against drunkenness and hard liquor but did not advocate for complete abstention. George Washington drank wine, with a hard leaning toward Madeira. Benjamin Franklin possessed a thousand bottles of French wine in his heyday. He often shared a bottle with John Adams. Dolly and James Madison had a thing for Pinot Noir. (Who could blame them?) And Thomas Paine was known to get one sip over the line. So where does the impulse to scold people into complete sobriety come from? Not from our founders. That much is clear.

Prohibition was driven, in part, by legitimate concerns. One was the availability of highly intoxicating and also cheap whisky, which could be distilled out of any number of affordable grains: wheat, oats, and, in particular, corn. Many drinkers abandoned their habit of drinking 2 percent beer for the habit of drinking whisky, which got men drunk quickly and cheaply.

A lot of this drinking took place in all-male saloons, often owned by local elected leaders who would shamelessly buy votes and hand out favors in their own saloons. In their documentary on Prohibition, Ken Burns and Lynn Novick report that "in 1890, eleven of New York City's twenty-four aldermen ran bars."[26] These saloons were mixed bags. Yes, they were rowdy. The noise emanating from them often frightened women and children who passed them on the sidewalk. Occasionally, a sober pedestrian had to step over or around an unconscious body just outside a saloon.

But saloons were also a social networking platform. Immigrant men could learn or improve their English in these havens, and they could often find employment and get translation services in the same saloon. Some saloons provided a place for homeless men to receive mail and read a free newspaper. They were informal meeting places for fraternities, unions, and groups of veterans. Historian Pete Hamill argues that saloons were integral to the survival of many immigrants. "They were the working-class private clubs," he notes.[27]

It is also true that drunkenness was and still is interwoven with domestic abuse. Advocates of total abstinence were rightly horrified by stories of men who would spend their paychecks at the bar and leave their children with no money for food that week. Drunkards were, and still are, known for beating their wives and traumatizing and abandoning their children.

The much-misunderstood Carrie Nation, born in Kentucky, was a victim of secondhand alcoholism. Her childhood had been unstable. As a result of her father's chronic illness, the family moved often, and her mother suffered from delusions, which included imagining that she was Queen Victoria.

Nation must have believed she found a safe haven with Charles Gloyd, a veteran Union fighter, doctor, and teacher. Gloyd was an alcoholic, but that did not stop him from marrying Caroline Amelia Moore (Carrie Nation) in 1867 when she was a few days away from her twenty-first birthday. They had been married less than a year when he died as a direct result of heavy drinking, and she was left with Charlien, their baby daughter. Luckily, she was not destitute and was able to leverage a small inheritance into a paid-off home and a teacher's certificate. She studied history and Greek philosophy at a normal institute in Missouri. Armed with these credentials, she took on the support of Gloyd's mother.

Despite being saddled with a child and mother-in-law, she managed to marry again, this time to David Nation, who was nineteen years older than she. Both of them worked in hotel management. What triggered Carrie Nation's first rampage was a new law that said other states could export booze to Kansas, in its original packaging. When she started destroying bars in Kiowa, Kansas, it was with the knowledge that many saloons were operating illegally, in defiance of Kansas blue laws. She could not have made the connection between male drunkenness and women's disempowerment more clearly when she stated, "You wouldn't give me the vote, so I had to use a rock!"[28] Many lawmen refused to arrest Nation, even after she had destroyed a saloon. In their hearts, they knew she was right. Drunkenness in husbands and fathers represented a terrible danger to women and children. And, in a country that struggles to provide a safety net for battered women, it still does.

Nation's activity looks both reasonable, within the context of the time and what she had endured, and trauma related at the same time. I would note that she had reached the age of fifty-three before she began her campaign as a direct activist. It is an age when cumulative trauma often catches up to people.

Nation's efficacy as a soldier for sobriety and women's rights was entirely effaced by an unsympathetic public who turned her into a caricature of righteous anger, the equivalent of a meme. She had no direct influence on Prohibition, which was ushered in mostly through the agency of Wayne B. Wheeler.

Women who ultimately supported Prohibition turned their earned wrath on saloons because of very real problems with husbands who drank to excess. However, the problem of the financially abandoned family is equally a women's issue. Women with little or no education and few if any marketable job skills will always be at the mercy of bad men.

One could argue—okay, I'm going to argue—that financial infidelity and abuse are better addressed by empowering women than by trying to reform men with restrictions. As we have seen in the twentieth and twenty-first centuries, women who make their own money and control their reproductive calendar do an impressive job of protecting themselves and their children.

Husbands are much less tempted to beat up fellow earners. As well, independent women can and will leave any man who fails to tow a line of basic decency. Where Prohibition failed utterly, improved opportunities for women have succeeded in producing a better class of men.

It would be unfair to say that the temperance movement was entirely motivated by racism and a fear of recent immigrants. But one of the key temperance players, the WCTU, was a predominantly white evangelical club that believed new immigrants from Europe needed training in order to become real Americans.

At one point, the leader of the WCTU explained that members needed to learn foreign languages and integrate themselves into the communities of these wayward immigrants, in order to educate them on how to act: "We must have a regiment of American workers, who will learn the German language, love the German people, work among the German children and young people until we get them to love clear brains better than beer," said WCTU president Bessie Laythe Scovell, in her 1900 speech to members.[29]

She went on to add that, similarly, some WCTU members must learn the Scandinavian languages and do the same kind of ministry to the wayward Nordic immigrants. Yet other club members would need to martyr themselves by learning the romance languages, *even Italian,* in order to infiltrate the southern European immigrant communities.

These missionaries of sobriety "must learn the French and Italian and various dialects, even, that the truths of personal purity and total abstinence be taught to these who dwell among us. We must feel it a duty to teach these people the English language to put them in sympathy with our purposes and our institutions."[30]

It must immediately be noted that the WCTU had many good intentions, including voting rights for women and the alleviation of poverty. They must also be credited with lobbying, successfully, to raise the age of sexual consent, both in the United States and in India; with installing public water fountains; and with advocating for free kindergarten education and equal pay for women.

By today's standards, however, the WCTU was hopelessly homogenous, and their overt presumption of superiority is mirrored in their failure to diversify their group. It is impossible to know whether Catholic women were actively discouraged from joining or simply wanted to stay as far away from these self-righteous do-gooders as possible. Either way, the WCTU point of view assumed the superiority of white Protestants, who practiced an extremist form of Christianity, a form of Christianity, it could be argued, that sets people up to fail.

Overall, the worst mistake of the WCTU was a failure to recognize that you can't stop humans from being humans. Nor did that group seriously contend with the psychology of addiction. To be fair, of course, science has made numerous useful discoveries about addiction, its hereditary nature, how one's environment supports or triggers those who are at the highest hereditary risk, and how drugs and alcohol change brain chemistry. These discoveries took place long after the efforts of WCTU to mitigate the worst effects of alcohol abuse.

While barring access to a recreational substance might work with people who can take or leave that substance in the first place, it never works with addicts. Addicts will simply find another, often more dangerous way to satisfy their craving. The textbook example of this would be the nice little old ladies who got hooked on opioids, prescribed by doctors, and ended up on heroin when they were cut off from their pills. And, no, I am not overdramatizing. On the side street where I lived for three years, there were two such addicts. One was found dead with a needle in her leg by her younger neighbor.

The ASL (Anti-Saloon League) was arguably the more powerful player in bringing about Prohibition. Leadership in that group was all male. The league recruited members from within churches and built up a substantial following.

The most important arm of the league was its printing company, called American Issue Publishing. Through its ownership of a print enterprise, which took up an entire city block in Westerville, Ohio, the league inundated citizens with magazines, newspapers, posters, pamphlets, songs, and dramatic narratives, all dedicated to spreading the word that booze of all kinds was dangerous and to be avoided completely.

Wayne B. Wheeler, head of the ASL, used anti-German sentiment that arose in World War I to draw a connection between the demon alcohol and those demon immigrants. Beer production at that time was dominated by the names of German families: Pabst, Busch, Schlitz. Wheeler subtly made the connection between these beer makers and treason.

One of the most troubling facts of Prohibition was its informal partnership with the Ku Klux Klan. "In the South, Prohibitionists stood side by side with racists whose living nightmare was the image of a black man with a bottle in one hand and a ballot in the other," writes Daniel Okrent.[31] "Support for Prohibition represented the single most important bond between Klansmen throughout the nation," wrote Leonard J. Moore in 1997.[32]

Historians have widely differing views of how well Prohibition worked, with some claiming that Prohibition jacked up drinking rates across the country. According to more moderate assessments, nationwide alcohol consumption during the Prohibition era was at about 70 percent of its pre-Prohibition rate due to medical use, religious use, home brewing, moonshining, and illegal trafficking.

Prohibitionists took that 30 percent overall decline as a solid win. However, in some urban areas, especially New York City, Prohibition drove consumption higher than it had been before the Eighteenth Amendment. The rise of organized crime was also clearly an unintended consequence of Prohibition.

In Kentucky, Prohibition turned the poor against one another. Frank A. Mather, a subsistence farmer, took a job as a federal agent in support of Prohibition. His annual salary of $1,500 would have greatly benefited his family, if he could have stayed alive in the job. While many such agents simply enriched themselves by taking bribes and looking the other way, Mather was an honest man whose entire family paid the price of his determination to do his job honorably.

Mather's short career as a federal agent illustrates a troubling inconsistency in the way Prohibition was enforced. Under the Eighteenth Amendment, it was not illegal to own alcoholic beverages, drink alcoholic beverages, or home brew alcohol for personal and family use. Wealthy whisky drinkers carefully stockpiled reserves for personal use.

One of the most famous of these evaders was J. B. Leonis, who hid his whisky library behind a wall of books in his official library. If you knew how to release the catch, the bookshelf would move out of the way and give access to expensive hooch. In 2018, Christie's auctioned off a number of bottles from this collection at formidably high prices.[33] Whisky was likewise stockpiled and kept safe by those who had licenses to sell it to pharmacies.

Out of sight, out of trouble was the principle at work, and wealthy wine and whisky drinkers could always afford to store their product out of sight. Subsistence moonshiners in Kentucky, however, did not enjoy that protection. Their storage facility was the woods. And when an agent could find a stockpile in those woods, he was authorized to take an axe to it.

Moonshine still owners had no recourse. There was no inquiry as to whether this hooch was for personal use. It could be destroyed with impunity. Federal agents, when they chose to do their jobs, were authorized to make a judgment call as to whether this stash was legal or illegal. They were judge and jury on their peers. The poor, therefore, got poorer while the wealthy aged their alcoholic product, making it more valuable.

Mather knew the hills of Kentucky, and he could often locate stills from observing where the smoke was rising above the trees. He and his sons, who often accompanied him, would find the hidden barrels in the forests. They dumped the contents, either mash or liquor, into a nearby waterway. Sometimes the moonshine would go into their truck's radiator to keep it from freezing up in the winter. For this, the Mathers were rewarded by having their barn burned down; a dog they were watching for a friend was shot.

Mather was one of several agents who raided the stills at Willie T. Thomas's residence. Eight people were arrested for violations of the Volstead Act. Mather and one other man were left alone to guard the arrestees while other agents left to do more raids. Several law officers showed up at the Thomas residence while Mather was guarding the violators. These fellow lawmen were already drunk and possibly hoped to continue drinking from Thomas's store. The confrontation between these two arms of the law quickly turned to violence. Mather was shot and died in the hospital the next day.[34]

Mather was by no means the only lawman to lose his life, violently, over liquor. The Lexington Police Department maintains an online memorial to J. J. Estes, who was shot and killed while pursuing a bootlegger on Kenton Street in 1927. He was thirty-three years old, and he left behind a widow, son, mother, and two siblings. His murderer was convicted and put in prison, then paroled in 1944.

While the Kentucky poor were being recruited to harass those even poorer in the name of Prohibition, bootlegger George Remus was building up his empire of legal and illegal booze sales. As a trained pharmacist, he was perfectly positioned to get rich on medicinal whisky. He operated legal pharmacies, which, under Prohibition, were given a dispensation to "prescribe" strong alcohol for medicinal purposes. Burns and Novick note that there were six million whisky prescriptions during the Prohibition era.[35] Whisky, not beer or wine.

Remus bought up distilleries that had been forced to close down, and he became a distiller himself. At the height of his power, he employed three thousand people. His staff would load up his trucks with whisky ostensibly destined for the pharmacies, then other Remus employees would overtake those trucks, rob them of a portion of their whisky, and divert the legally distilled whisky to speakeasies and elsewhere that Prohibition was being flouted. One hopes that the employees manning the illegal trucks were paid a higher wage. If they were arrested, they were on their own.

Remus sold whisky made in two Kentucky distilleries: the Old Pogue and Hill & Hill. The Old Pogue had been established in 1876 in Maysville, Kentucky. Remus never legally acquired the Old Pogue; instead, the distillery made whisky and sold it to Remus. Bourbon had been made in that region for decades previous. Before Kentucky was even a state, ambitious frontiersmen discovered how well corn and limestone water combined to make a powerful inebriant.

In 1920, Remus bought the equally historic Hill & Hill distillery in Owensboro, Kentucky, for $320,000, equivalent to over $4 million today. Hill & Hill, also known as Rock Springs Distilling Co., had been established by the Hill brothers in 1881.

Ironically, George Remus is sometimes credited with "saving" bourbon from disappearing as a result of Prohibition. The truth, as it usually is, was more complex. Remus had a license to sell medicinal whisky because he was a pharmacist. But other Kentucky distilleries were also able to get licenses. The bigger and more well known the distillery, the more likely it was to receive a license.

American Medicinal Spirits, A. Ph. Stitzel, Frankfort Distilleries, Glenore, Old Forester, and Schenley were able to sell the bourbon they had already manufactured, pre-Prohibition, under the medicinal licenses. They were also free to buy whisky from other distillers who were storing their pre-Prohibition product.

When the distilleries ran out of whisky, an emergency 1929 dispensation allowed them to make more bourbon for everyone who could afford to bribe a doctor. Though the income from prescriptions did not equal pre-Prohibition income, it was enough to keep those distilleries alive, while smaller, family-owned businesses shuttered, never to reopen. Most of the six Kentucky distilleries, which provided medicinal bourbon under their own licenses, have been bought out or merged into other corporations. The exception is Old Forester.

But there was no Volstead Act loophole to save Kentucky's wine industry. Though Missouri's wine started coming back in the 1960s, Kentucky didn't get serious about making wine until the 1990s when government incentives finally encouraged it.

Prohibition was not uniformly bad for Kentucky. The city of Newport, Kentucky, currently part of greater metropolitan Cincinnati, savvily declared itself an "independent municipality," unaffiliated with county, state, and country. The intent was clear. Newport intended to become wealthy by flouting the Volstead Act. And so, it did.

With the help of at least two powerful gangsters, George Remus and Pete Schmidt, Newport became an early version of Las Vegas. Whisky, beer, and wine flowed generously in speakeasies, casinos opened, sex workers plied their trade, and "gentlemen" enjoyed stripteases.

A-list entertainment followed the money. According to Chez Chesak of the *Los Angeles Times*, before the Rat Pack was even a thing, Frank Sinatra and Jerry Lewis performed in Newport, as did Sammy Davis Jr., Marilyn Monroe, Bob Hope, Jack Benny, and the Marx Brothers.[36] At the tender age of seventeen, Dean Martin worked there as a bartender's assistant. Newport's nickname was "Sin City," and it became a template for the development of other gambling towns.

The repeal of Prohibition, which drastically changed so many institutions, left Newport mostly untouched. It continued happily merchandising "sin" right up to the beginning of the 1960s. In '61, Kentucky governor Bert Combs discovered that Newport was, in fact, part of Kentucky, despite decades of bravado over its self-declared independence. Under Combs's administration, Newport would have to start abiding by state law, the governor declared. Rather belatedly, one might think, he sent lawmen to raid the casinos. The newly minted attorney general Robert F. Kennedy directed the Justice Department to investigate and arrest mobsters, especially those flagrantly operating in Newport. The flapper era in Newport came to a late end, and today there is nary a casino there.

In Kentucky, Prohibition did not end tidily in 1933. Instead of celebrating their freedom, many counties opted to remain dry, and moonshining continued apace, accounting for many shoot-outs and deaths, mostly of lawmen. One has to wonder if the moonshiners themselves voted to keep rural Kentucky counties dry as a way of protecting their business interests. The demand for moonshine would almost certainly decline if dry county residents could buy some drama-free whisky in a store. Instead, dry county residents risked the blindness and paralysis that could result from drinking unregulated whisky that was too strong or contaminated. And moonshiners continued to make a profit, on which they neither paid taxes nor endured health inspections.

Tobacco farming in Kentucky was already a growing industry before Prohibition. With the bourbon, wine, and beer industries largely shuttered, it was natural for farmers who had produced corn for whisky to convert their land to tobacco production. Tobacco was a lucrative crop, and Kentucky still ranks first and second among the United States in tobacco production, first for burley and second for total tobacco.

Replacing alcohol with tobacco is ethically problematic, as most readers probably know. According to the World Health Organization, tobacco kills around six million people annually, while alcohol-related deaths total 2.5 million. C. Everett Koop authored a publication declaring that cigarettes kill more people than alcohol, AIDS, vehicular accidents, fire, murder, cocaine, crack, and heroin combined.[37] By trading grape arbors for tobacco fields, Kentucky's government was killing its own and other states' people much more efficiently than George Remus or Al Capone had ever done.

If anyone thinks alcohol restrictions in Kentucky have ever actually produced a more sober state population, I would very much like to see the data. What we have as a reward for all the dry counties is an opioid epidemic. As of 2015, Kentucky ranked third in the nation for most opioid-related deaths in the United States. By 2022, West Virginia had pulled ahead of us in fatal drug overdoses, but Kentucky still ranked in the top four.

In 1976, Kentucky's legislature very belatedly tried to correct the course. In that year, Kentucky lawmakers determined that the state could make wine once more. Funds for tobacco farming were diverted to grape growers. But that legislation was far too late and also too little, because grape growing came with a cap on production. As late as 2018, Purple Toad Winery in Paducah complained that limits on wine production were threatening their expansion.[38]

In that same year, the risks from methamphetamine production in Kentucky were already quite clear. By 2019, Kentucky was in the top six states producing meth. Laws restricting the purchase of Sudafed, an ingredient in conventional meth production, drove producers to concoct the drug using phenyl-2-propanone, or P2P. P2P can be produced using a number of different liquids; meth cookers no longer have to buy suspicious amounts of any one product. According to the *Atlantic Monthly*, the "new meth," using P2P, is both more dangerous to make and also more dangerous for the user.[39]

In 2023, Craig Dupree Robertson of Lexington, Kentucky, was found guilty of running a giant meth and fentanyl sales team. Perhaps the ghosts of Prohibition leaders, so scared of the all-male saloons, took comfort in knowing that four of Robertson's ten coconspirators were women.

On a late May weekend, Joel and I made the two-hour trip to Bracken County, Kentucky, once a flourishing wine capital that produced half the nation's wine. The drive there took us through some nearly pristine forest along the southern bank of the Ohio.

"I can see why the Europeans who came here fell in love with this place," Joel remarked. He was right. Except for the tarmacked road, we could have been in that virginal moment of the Ohio River Valley's history. All the ensuing pollution, industry, and overdevelopment of this region have left few marks on this particular stretch of State Highway 8. There are few residences and fewer businesses. Instead, there is a surprising diversity of trees and other florae, along with glimpses of the river, which, from that distance, looks perfectly blue and untroubled. At many points, the valley looks much as it would have looked to Dufour, Longworth, and Abe Baker. I was eager to see the Baker-Bird Winery because the wine cellar there, built by Abraham Baker, is the oldest in the country. Much of the Kentucky wine produced in the late 1800s was made there.

I was also eager to meet Dinah Bird, the winemaker who saved the Baker-Bird Winery from being bulldozed on behalf of a wider road. When I caught up to her, she was multitasking: making crepes on a ridiculously small device and fielding the myriad questions that her visitors had. She studied viticulture in California. A few seconds spent stalking her on social media also show that she holds a PhD and has a second (or first) career as an estate planner.

In person, the first thing she told me was that her husband considers the winery a "money pit." As she struggled a little to produce the number of ham and cheese crepes her clients were demanding, she also said she was "robbing Peter to pay Paul."

Bird acts as a consultant for the region's vineyards on a volunteer basis and gets the first pick of grapes. From these, she makes several different wines, but I was surprised not to see Norton on the tasting menu. It turned out that Baker-Bird does make a sweet wine that is part Norton, but I settled on a glass of Thunder Bolt, which is a Cabernet aged in barrels that held bourbon for nine years. I learned from the Baker-Bird website that the heat produced on the back of my palate by the Thunder Bolt bourbon base note is called a "Kentucky hug." Baker-Bird is also making a Cabernet Franc and a Vidal Blanc that, according to Bird, is the most commonly planted wine grape in Kentucky. The grounds are magnificent, the cellar beautifully etched by time, and spruced up with red chrysanthemums as many wineries in this area are. There are fliers inviting people to schedule their events here, especially weddings. You definitely want your wedding at Baker-Bird.

I found myself a little troubled by how often wineries supplement income from their principal business by staging events. But, upon a little sager reflection, who am I to say how any winery should make its money? What would be really horrible would be if I couldn't get a glass of wine that wasn't made in California by some huge, heartless corporation. If family wineries need multiple revenue streams to stay in business, I should applaud their ingenuity. And drink their wine.

Bird relayed that the hard Kentucky winters of 2013 and 2014 killed a lot of grapevines in Bracken County and nearby. Many of the Cab Francs survived, but the Vidal Blanc vines took three years to recover, she told me. The tech and knowledge for producing French grapes in America have improved, but it still feels like wineries that grow Cab Franc and Vidal, both French varietals, are sort of repeating the mistakes of Jefferson, Dufour, and Longworth. Again.

After centuries have proven you can't grow those grapes here. Not consistently. I was surprised not to find Vignoles at any of the Kentucky wineries. I'm not an agrarian scientist, but it feels like the weather in Kentucky could be no worse than in Missouri, where Vignoles is growing like mad.

Straight down Route 8 is another historic winery called StoneBrook. The road into it is badly eroded, but picturesque. There are separate parking lots for cars and horses. StoneBrook is on a popular and well-promoted wine trail, and it was busy on a Saturday afternoon.

Our sommelier was way too busy to talk to us. The winery does grow its own Norton, he said, so I got a glass of that. It was a little medicinal, which seems to be the peril of making a Norton, but it was still a solid table wine. I can see why winemakers recommend it with red meat. Many versions of Norton need to pair with a hearty food that can balance it.

The tasting menu featured a number of fruity and sweet wines, including a pineapple mead. There is some really good mead circulating around Kentucky and Indiana, so I was hopeful about the mead, but "I've had better meads," Joel pronounced. My bias says that mead should be leggy, legs for miles, and this mead was thin.

Our next stop was Prodigy, a winery twenty miles outside of Lexington and within shooting distance of Frankfort, Kentucky's capital. I was slightly surprised to find what can only be described as a neighborhood bar on site. Sports were blaring from a television, and eyes that had grown bored with the beautiful horse country just outside the huge windows were trained on the game. Both Bud and Miller Lite were on the menu, along with pizza and crackers. This is a good place for wine drinkers to take their beer and sports friends as a compromise, I guess. Again, I had to remind myself that a winery making its own wine in Kentucky is a major win. Whatever they have to do to succeed is a good thing.

Behind the bar is a gift and souvenir shop that sells a hodgepodge of T-shirts, derby hats, and tea towels embossed with sentiments like "Drink up, bitches." Our bartender informed us that the grapes for Prodigy's Norton wine come from nearby Lawrenceburg.

Our tasting of four wines came in a row of science beakers. My Norton would definitely have paired well with a cheeseburger, but I liked the Chambourcin better. Prodigy's Chambourcin, according to the menu, won

Commissioner's Cup awards for best dry red in Kentucky in both 2013 and 2017. My favorite of the tasting was the red Zinfandel, however.

Prodigy's port is Norton based and fortified with brandy, as all port must be to be called port. It goes by the name Legacy Estate Port. Nicholas Longworth would approve of the attempted status inflation. It is a wine to be proud of. It is delicious, with beautiful layering. The Norton is a recognizable base note. The sweet high notes presumably come from other vintages.

Joel thought the semisweet Traminette would pair well with whitefish. For some reason, it made me yearn for a vegan black bean chili. The blueberry wine, made with real blueberry juice, as opposed to flavoring, was a surprise, as it was a white wine. Remembering Nicholas Longworth, Joel asked, "Did they get a bunch of low-wage employees to peel the blueberries?"

I was especially eager to see the Wildside Winery, also close to Lexington, because the vineyard grew out of an organic farm, and the owners, Neil Vasilakes and his wife, Rebecca, remain committed to using as few chemicals as possible. Neil's degree from the University of Minnesota is in mechanical engineering. The couple left Minnesota and moved to Kentucky, at least in part to escape the brutal winters. They bought their acres in the late 1990s and planted their fruit before even building their house. According to the winery website, the thirty acres they purchased were entirely fallow, "nothing but cattle paths and tobacco stubs."[40]

In the tradition of Dufour, they started out with a wine club. Friends and friends of friends would gather to share the work of making wine, make a lot of wine, then share out the costs. Eventually, this turned into a business, which has expanded over time.

They are not self-taught winemakers, exactly, but their training was a little random, a class here, a book there. They learned a lot from other local winemakers and growers, proving that making interesting wines might be more about determination than study. They have expanded several times, and they grow a variety of grape species, a little something for everyone.

Joel pointed to a Tempranillo on the menu and said, "Why?" I must have contaminated him, though I confess to thinking a Rioja is a bit of a stretch for Kentucky. Still, diversifying grapes protects a vineyard in the event that disease or cold takes one species.

As we approached the tasting room on a Sunday, a loud and spirited band playing live music assailed our ears. The inside of the winery is redolent of a roadside tavern: lots of wood, lots of noise. The grounds are gorgeous, a deck with trellised nooks inviting lovers to nestle together and look out at the grapevines and the nearby woods. It was a beautiful spring day, and I could definitely see why a young couple would want to have a June wedding in that setting.

It was also busy with patrons crowding around the stage and spilling outside. The crowd at Wildside reminded me of that Billy Joel verse "The regular crowd shuffles in." If they were not all regulars, they were definitely treating the place as a familiar watering hole. It occurred to me that, if Kentucky restaurants and package stores don't want to support local and regional wines, Kentuckians are actually prepared to go to the wine.

The Wildside Norton was a good one, definitely something you want to pair with protein. The cheddar and almonds that we put on the side of our wine paired really well and brought out latent dimensions. You would not want to pair that Norton with a cucumber and watermelon salad. It needs strong tastes to balance it.

Prodigy and Wildside have shown that independent wineries in Kentucky can succeed by diversifying. Live music, inviting bars, beautiful decks, event hosting, a location near to a city but far enough out that city dwellers feel they're "getting away from it all." This combination of assets may put Kentucky back on the wine map one day.

4
Hermann Rises Again

The day Joel and I visited the Adam Puchta Winery was a perfect day in May. Ours was the only car on the narrow winding road that took us there. Towering oak and hickory trees threw dappled shade on the entrance as we approached. The Frene Creek runs across the Puchta property at the visitor entrance. The buildings there go back to Adam Puchta's time. Except for the car on the road, we could have been approaching a German winery during the heydays of German winemaking in Missouri's Ohio Valley.

"So this is where they make Cynthiana," Joel said.

"Norton, Honey. They call it Norton here," I said. "There's a war."

Well, not a war. That's poetic license. But there's a debate over whether Norton and Cynthiana are the same grape, despite DNA studies that *strongly* suggest they are the exact same grape. And, if they are, what should that grape be called? In Missouri, winemakers and consumers call it "Norton," observing the origins of the wine on Daniel Norton's farm. In Arkansas, they call it "Cynthiana." More on that later.

The fact of the genetic similarities between Norton and Cynthiana is actually quite exciting. As of this writing, the most recent report on Norton's DNA comes from late in 2023. It suggests that today's Norton and Cynthiana wines are essentially derived from a native grape, accidentally hybridized with Meslier Petit, a European grape that is now rarely grown.[1]

Missouri's state grape is Norton, and Missouri winemakers have been making Norton wines for going on two centuries, using wine processes brought over from Germany. The hub of Missouri wine is Hermann, the seat of Gasconade County, which makes many claims to greatness.

The Adam Puchta Winery is the unbroken link between the past and present of winemaking in Hermann, Missouri. Named after the nineteenth-century winemaker Adam Puchta, the winery claims to be the oldest family-owned winery in continuous existence in the United States. Adam was still a child when his parents and siblings moved from Bavaria to Missouri in 1839. Unlike many of the Missouri settlers who eventually became grape growers out of necessity, Adam's father, John Henry Puchta, was an experienced winemaker who bought his acres in the Frene Creek Valley with the express purpose of viniculture.

Adam and his brother Frederick Puchta joined a band of young men headed west to California to join the gold rush. They wisely provisioned themselves with a herd of cattle. Upon arrival, they sold this herd to set themselves up as prospectors.

Adam lived in California for two years, then traveled to Nicaragua, where he continued prospecting for gold. If youth must have adventures, Adam certainly fulfilled that cliché. According to the Adam Puchta Winery website, he walked the entire length of Panama on his return to Hermann.[2]

What does wealth profit a man if he cannot return to his hometown and flaunt it, just a little? Adam may have left home a dreamer and speculator, but he returned as a solid businessman with a plan.

The Adam Puchta website leaves some gaps in history, not the least of which is whether Adam returned to Hermann a rich man. What we do know is that he wasted no time in buying some acres from his father, then building a stone cellar and winepress house. The Puchtas transitioned from being grape farmers to farmers, vintners, and wine merchants. Norton was among the grapes they grew, fermented, and bottled.

In 1855, only sixteen years after the family's arrival in Missouri, the Puchta family had barreled its first vintages. By the 1870s, the Puchta name was well established as a quality wine brand.

In the 1880s, Adam's son Henry joined him in the business, which was renamed Adam Puchta & Son Wine Co. Puchta wines were sold all over Missouri, to tavern owners and individuals. The business passed to Henry and his son Everett but had to close in 1919 due to Prohibition.

A little-known loophole in Prohibition allows the Adam Puchta Winery to claim continuous production. Under the Volstead Act, commercial wineries and distilleries were closed down, but families and individuals could make their own wine, beer, or cider for personal use, up to two hundred gallons a year per household.

The Puchtas kept their equipment in use and maintained their skills by making wine for personal use. They turned some of their farmland to different purposes. Some Norton grapevines, hidden in a forest, escaped the attention of the feds, as did some commercial winemaking equipment that the family hid under straw piles. That equipment has survived to this day.

The Puchtas did not immediately return to commercial winemaking after the repeal of Prohibition in 1933. But they preserved the facilities, processing wine for family and friends, until 1990 when Puchta descendants decided to revive their family's heritage business. Henry Puchta's grandson Randy and his son, Timothy, went into winemaking together and produced a thousand gallons their first year.

It is, perhaps, a happy coincidence that, in the 1990s, the consumption of red wine doubled in the United States. More than one historian has theorized that the ascendancy of wine in America, especially red wine, comes down to a *60 Minutes* episode in which Morley Safer talked about the "French paradox."[3]

The French paradox has the French consuming just as much fat as Americans but having way fewer heart attacks. Safer suggested it was the red wine that the French were drinking. This message was music to the ears of baby boomers who had reduced their alcohol consumption while raising their children, but who now longed for a good reason to season their middle and late years with a little booze. And here, in the nick of time, comes Morley Safer to tell them that wine is good for you, if only it's red!

(The French paradox is an ongoing enigma, but the red wine theory has been pretty well discredited by health pros. Turns out it's not so much the fat in our food that will stop a heart; it's the fat around our middles. Even in France, obesity is on the rise, but that population is still at only 17 percent obesity, while 40 percent of Americans are obese. The mystery here is not heart attacks—it's why the French stay so skinny. This is such a troubling disparity that someone actually measured how long the French take to eat dinner and noticed they take more time between bites. They make conversation and eye contact during their meals, like an actual civilization. Could slow eating be the great cure for obesity?

Well. It's more likely to be cities engineered to encourage walking.

Meanwhile, doctors are begging Americans not to have more than two small drinks a day of any kind. Liver cirrhosis is also going to kill a significant quantum of us. "All things in moderation" might be the best guideline the Greek philosophers ever gave.

But the message of red wine's miraculous health benefits, like any closest cliché, has irrevocably settled in the American consciousness and is unlikely to move on any time soon.)

It's impossible to quantify the effect that a *60 Minutes* episode had on the success of the Adam Puchta Winery revival. But production there has grown to seventy-five thousand gallons a year and is poised to expand quite a bit further under the leadership of Parker Puchta.

Timothy Puchta has now spent most of his adult life making wine, and his son, Parker Puchta, joined him in the business. When we visited in May 2023, Parker was running the winery, and he represents the seventh generation of winemaking Puchtas. Parker's older brother, Spencer, lends an occasional hand.

Missourians can trace their Norton grapes back to Dr. Daniel Norton, by way of Cincinnati. So it makes sense to call it Norton. I'm coming to terms with the plain-Janeness of the name. It is not a plain wine. Perhaps it is enough to let the Norton layers speak for themselves, and I don't have to attempt to twist language to suit my sensibilities.

My husband, Joel, took a vacation week with me to visit Hermann and talk Norton with anyone who wanted to talk Norton. His presence elevated this trip from a needful but lonely sojourn to a spring break in Paris. He is the love of my life. I don't understand how people tire of a well-chosen spouse. We have been together for twenty-five years. He ages like good wine. I decant a little of him every day and savor the complex layers of monogamy.

We had bought tickets for the "elevated wine tasting" at Adam Puchta in advance. I should now confess that I thought this experience would be a little touristy, maybe a little tired in the way that destination events often become. I was wrong.

The tastings take place in the former winepress; antique equipment is on display. It is a beautiful room, all wood and filtered light. It has the kind of charm you would want for a family reunion. It would be difficult to quarrel in those surroundings.

Our tasting station was beautifully set with a gorgeous charcuterie platter and Riedel glassware from Austria. Our sommelier, Lee Baker, explained that Riedel has now designed a glass specifically for Norton wine. It is the first wineglass designed specifically for a native American vintage. Wine enthusiasts in a stratum far above me swear by Riedel glasses and maintain that they enhance the flavor of the wine. They are worth the cost of seventy to one hundred dollars a glass, connoisseurs believe. My thrift store glassware suddenly seemed a little random, but I quickly consoled myself by remembering my low credit card balance.

The charcuterie was selected with the Nortons in mind. The lightly dotted espresso cheese paired perfectly with the dry, complex vintage, as did the hard salami and chocolate truffles. Most everything on our plate had been handpicked from local or regional sources. I came to regret my carb loading at Waffle House, a face stuffing that began with the words "We can't afford to drink wine for breakfast on an empty stomach."

Despite my often sober judgment, I had signed up for the 11 a.m. tasting.

Lee was heavily accessorized; as she handled the wine bottles, I could see that this was deliberate. Each wine was presented to us in a jeweled setting, formed by rings and a bracelet, all in wine colors. Up one of her arms, there was a tattoo of a grapevine. There was a level of commitment to her profession that you rarely see.

I got a little of Lee's story, just enough to understand that she is one of those women destined to succeed at whatever she applies herself to. She and her husband lived next door to a winery. She walked over and asked for a job. Part-time turned into full-time. Parker recruited her for Adam Puchta. I afforded him some unspoken congratulations on talent spotting.

I was nervous about bringing my laptop to this tasting; when Lee saw me taking notes on the menu, she brought me a pad of writing paper. I wish she worked for me.

Our first sample was a reserve Vignoles. This might be a good time to confess that I don't have a broad wine vocabulary. "Wow" was what I came up with. The Vignoles was really, really good. There was a strong hint of pineapple that I tasted in all the Vignoles we had in Hermann. Almost as if someone dropped a ring of pineapple in your glass. And yet, this white wine was fairly dry. Joel was similarly impressed.

"I don't think I've had a Vignoles before, or I forgot," I ventured.

"We would have remembered this," he said, emphatically.

I know enough of Vignoles to know that it is fast becoming a favorite of vineyard growers and winemakers outside of California. In Virginia, the agriculture gurus are pushing it as *the* grape.

Vignoles is another mystery of the wine world, more so even than Norton/Cynthiana. A Frenchman of the name J. F. Ravat claimed to have hybridized a hybrid grape with a clone grape, and he named it after himself. For a time, that grape was called Ravat 51. Ravat 51 was supposedly imported to the United States, where it was renamed "Vignoles" by the Finger Lakes Wine Growers Association.

Until rather recently, it was a product of the Finger Lakes region. Neither Ravat 51 nor Vignoles is grown much in Europe. Despite its very French-sounding name, Vignoles is an American wine, frequently referred to as a "French-American" vintage by grape growers.

And here's the rub: J. F. Ravat was a renowned grape breeder who could, we might hope, be trusted to tell the truth about a grape varietal that he developed. What he told us about the ancestry of Ravat 51 was that he crossed the Le Subereux grape with Pinot de Corton, a descendant of Pinot Noir.

Yet a twenty-first-century genetic analysis found none of that ancestry in the Vignoles that is being grown all over the Midwest, Southeast, and Northeast. That might bear some unpacking. Several scientists from the University of California, Davis, and one from Cornell did a DNA analysis of America's Vignoles. There were existing Le Subereux and Pinot de Corton grapes to compare to our Vignoles grapes. Scientists almost never want to declare anything in absolute terms, so it was surprising that they concluded, emphatically, that the presumed parents of Vignoles could not be the parents of Vignoles.[4] Vignoles, my dear readers, might have started life as a bastard or even a hoax.

According to the DNA study, conducted in France, Vignoles is a descendant of two wines developed by Albert Seibel, a botanist and grape designer of status approximately equal to Ravat.[5] My attempts to learn the exact ancestry of Vignoles hit several dead ends. One of Vignoles' parents, a wine called Plantet, is also of uncertain parentage.

But this is interesting: Albert Seibel liked to cross French vines with American vines, and he kept using the same four vines in a series of breeding experiments. Two of those vines were *Vitis rupestris* and *Vitis lincecumii*. *Rupestris* is a native American grape, most valued for its hardy rootstock. *Lincecumii* is a wild American grape that I had not heard of, so I looked it up on the Lady Bird Johnson Wildflower Center website. According to that site, *Vitis lincecumii* is a variety of *Vitis aestivalis*, the grape that Norton is based on.[6]

Could Vignoles be a Cynthiana/Norton wine or a close relative? Is that why it's so delicious? Is that why it grows so well in Virginia?

Never mind. This is the land of opportunity, Horatio Alger, and the birthplace of democracy. If we are anything, we are capable of judging a grape on the basis of its merit, not its pedigree. If she looks like a lady and acts like a lady, she must be a lady. If anything, the suggestion of a hidden past adds to the flavor.

I have mixed feelings, though. Is Vignoles going to push Norton further over on the sidelines where it has lived so much of its life? If America falls in love with Vignoles, which is hardy and can grow in so many places, will there still be room for Norton?

I need not have worried. As good as the Vignoles was, Adam Puchta's reserve bourbon barrel Norton was even better. It's the kind of wine that would tempt you to pass on heaven, harps, angels, and all.

"Thank you, but, if it's all the same, I'm just going to sit here and sip on the Norton," I hear myself tell an angry rapture angel.

Someone from the winery described it as "silky rich, full mouth." It's also 19 percent alcohol. To put that into correct context, a French Bordeaux or Burgundy hovers at around 13 percent, as do the Italian Chianti and Spanish Rioja. No wonder I'm so fond of American wines!

Everywhere I go, people assure me that the Norton pairs well with red meat, steak, lamb, and burgers, as befits a wine pioneered by rugged German poets and philosophers who somehow ended up in Missouri. It's also really lovely with sharp cheddar, which is more likely to be in my fridge than the slaughtered mammals.

I had hoped that Parker would show up some time during our tasting, and he did, apologizing for his sweat. "We wouldn't really believe you owned a vineyard if you were clean," I assured him. I'm self-taught as to social skills, so I never know if I'm being appropriate.

He had just bought a new crush pad that would allow the winery to process fifteen tons of grapes at a time, in contrast to the five tons they could process before. Adam Puchta was poised to increase its output by 200 percent. Parker was also signed up for a class on how to control wine acidity. He was also responsible for the bistro attached to the winery. Expanding that to a full-size restaurant was on his agenda.

I asked him about the age of the Norton grapes; are they pre-Prohibition? He diverted me to a discussion of the wild grapes growing up trees in the woods outside the vineyard. He suspected they are Concord, but the University of Missouri was slated to do an analysis.

No opportunity should be overlooked. This is a man in whom the future of Norton is safe. I can exhale.

As of this writing, Parker is quite a young man. When he was even younger, he left home, as young men do. He studied culinary arts, not winemaking, which surprised me a little. He apprenticed as a chef in an upscale restaurant. He came back to Hermann in 2015 to run his family's business. He describes himself as self-taught in wines; he grew up around wine and winemakers who taught him. He has been learning how to make and market wines since he was a child.

The bourbon barrel Norton was the best of our elevated tasting, but the 2010 and 2011 Nortons, with their amber tinge, also grew on me rather quickly. Lee pointed out that the Puchta wines are all fruit forward, a wine assessment that I could actually taste. No "oak bombs" here. She joked that some wines are so oaky, it's like chewing on a tree.

The bourbon Norton started with Parker. "I have a lot of friends who drink bourbon," he explained casually. He was quick to note, however, that he himself does not drink strong spirits. He took the idea of Norton aged in bourbon barrels to his winemakers, and they ran with it. He couldn't say where the barrels come from because of some kind of nondisclosure agreement, but he did say they come from "Nashville." A quick romp through the internet shows that Nashville is home to several barrel companies. Who knew?

Parker is not the kind of man who works on having good narratives. But he has good ideas, which is more to the point, and ambitions. As Lee proves, he also has an infallible instinct for hiring good people.

I was glad we ponied up for the elevated tasting, because it turns out the bourbon barrel Norton is available only to wine club members, according to Lee. It might get served at one or more vertical dinners. Vertical wine dinners, I am learning, are dinners at which the same wine is presented throughout the meal, but different years of the same wine are paired with different dishes.

I am fascinated with the wine club model of sales because it echoes the wine societies of the nineteenth century. Jean Jacques Dufour started up America's first wine industry in Kentucky by forming a wine society. It was a strategy for raising start-up costs. People paid up front for wine that would be produced, at least initially, for the society's members. It is similarly a model for community-supported agriculture, which, in a very real way, is what an independent vineyard is.

What I did not know when I started writing this book is that wine societies still exist. They fly under the radar, one of the largely unknown perks of extreme wealth. Membership in the Commanderie de Bordeaux costs approximately $1,000 a year. But just having more money than sense is not enough to get in. Prospective members also have to take a written and oral test of their wine knowledge and host a dinner for existing members. This is not the 4-H.

The society's website does not tell people how to become members, but there is a daunting online form that I know better than to fill out and submit. I have never once received a reply to an online contact form. There are 1,200 U.S. members of the Commanderie de Bordeaux, a figure that seems low, considering how desirable the wine must be. But that figure makes the 180 members of the Adam Puchta Winery seem more respectable.

Château Gloria proprietor Henri Martin started up the Commanderie in 1959 as a way of increasing exports to the United States after World War II. The first chapter was in New York, and now there are eighty chapters across the world. The closest one to my old Kentucky home is in Nashville. Honestly, I don't really aspire to be in a wine society. But the Puchta wine club has a great deal of appeal. There shall be no deliveries of bourbon barrel Norton or any other Puchta wine for Lynn, though, because most vineyards don't ship to Kentucky. Adam Puchta uses VinoShipper, which ships to thirty-nine states, including Hawaii and Alaska. But not Kentucky.

The non-shipment to Kentucky astonished every winery I stopped at. Some states have so many dry counties that it's just not logistically viable to ship to them, the winemakers and sommeliers explain. But that can't be the problem in Kentucky, they are sure of that. They have seen the Lexington racehorses and julep drinkers on television, and they imagine Kentucky is more sophisticated than it actually is. They have not been to eastern Kentucky. We have dry counties galore.

A question that has been haunting me is: Just who are the people who buy Norton online? St. Louis is two hours away. Are there penthouse dwellers there, sipping Norton and looking out their windows at the cityscape, congratulating themselves on their originality? Because you have to be well into wine to order it online and not just pick it up in a package store.

To order wine from a small, independent winery, you mostly have to have a taste for a specific, small-batch wine. This requires the buyer to have not just money for noncorporate wines but also experience of such wines and a fair determination not to be swayed by what the masses like. Yet Adam Puchta is *not* just a tourist destination, getting by on its historic heritage and selling experiences. At least 40 percent of the winery's income comes from direct sales of wine, Parker says. They sell a lot of wines to fellow Missourians, but they also have a solid percentage of product going to Chicago. The bistro and tastings provide the other income streams.

Parker told me that the wineries work together so that all can succeed. In 2022, Adam Puchta loaned some equipment to the winery down the road. I'm speculating that this cooperation is why Hermann, overall, seems to be thriving in an era when so many small midwestern towns are dying. Teenagers pack their bongs, leave for college, and are rarely if ever seen again in many struggling heartland towns.

Joel and I stayed upstairs at the Piano Bar in Hermann, a very central location, walkable to several wineries. Across from the Piano Bar are the more expensive Hermann Crown Suites, and it was pleasant to see a proud window display of local wines, Norton prominent, on the ground floor of that hotel. It was even more of a thrill to see an online review complaining that a Hermann convenience store was selling a local wine at a cheaper price than the winery was selling it. Proof that local businesses are supporting one another *and* that the locals want the same wines that people travel to Hermann to taste and buy. Now, if the rest of the world would just start supporting local products.

In many ways, Hermann, Missouri, is the utopia it was supposed to be. It is unusually clean; the sidewalks and roads are in good condition; municipal buildings, businesses, and residences are all well maintained. There were no signs of homelessness or addiction, and all the residents seemed to feel safe. It's a model midwestern town, but without the Stepford creepiness. If the Hermann Wurst Haus is any indication, the biggest problem they have in Hermann is with tourists.

Upon entering the Wurst Haus, we saw a large sign that said "Free Samples" with a big black X over those words. Clearly, that system of generosity got played one too many times by cynical freeloaders. On the door of the Wurst Haus was another sign praising the business's staff and asking clients not to "crush their spirits" with rudeness and also inviting those who think they can do a better job to fill out an application. Signs of a post-COVID world.

We were lunching at the Wurst Haus, in Hermann's business district, because Joel noticed I was shaking badly, an outcome of excitement combined with low blood sugar. Wurst Haus is an enormous store with a high ceiling, reminiscent of a Viking hunting lodge. Over the men's room is mounted the head of an antlered stag; the stag's wife did not escape the hunters either. Her head is over the ladies' room. I didn't really expect to have one of the best meals of my life there, and that goes to show that nothing is what it seems. The food was world class. Wurst Haus wurst has won multiple awards, some in Germany.

We ordered the German platter to share, and it came with the "best of show" bratwurst, which was delicious, but pretty much what you would expect. Less predictable and utterly fabulous was the pear and gorgonzola wurst. We couldn't decide between the deviled egg potato salad and the German potato salad, so we got both, and they were similarly awesome.

It was the best German food I have ever had in my life. It was the best German food Joel had ever had, and he couldn't resist joking that the German food in Hermann was so much better than the German food in Germany. We spent a week in East Berlin, ten years after the wall came down, navigating terrible food. By the time Joel had received two raw potatoes at two different restaurants, we developed a stronger survival sense and only dined at the curry restaurants. Hopefully, German tourist food has improved in the years since.

I was curious to see what kind of wines the Wurst Haus had. The wines were lined up in refrigerators with glass doors. They looked like convenience store soda fridges, so my heart sank a little. It sprung back up, though, when it turned out that one whole fridge was dedicated to Adam Puchta wine. The gentleman behind the counter didn't know what I meant by "Norton," even though his wife was one of the Puchta wine club members.

Happily, I spotted a Hunter's Red, a Norton blend, as I knew from my research. I have to admit that the claims of how well Norton pairs with red meat were all true. It went wonderfully with my wurst and potatoes.

Once we had established a platform of carbs and protein, it was time to continue the wine tasting, this time at the estimable Stone Hill Winery, the legacy of Michael Poeschel. The Stone Hill vineyards range along the hills near Hermann's town center. The winery is smack in the middle of a beautiful residential neighborhood. I am a little jealous, especially of the folks whose large deck backs right up to the grape rows. These people can stroll uphill, buy a world-class bottle of wine, unique to American history, then drink it on their deck, looking out on a vineyard. They literally live inside a wine tasting.

The Stone Hill tastings take place at the far end of the winery's gorgeous retail space. Like the Wurst Haus, the style of architecture could be described as Viking hall, aspiring to capture Valhalla. The ceilings are high; shiny wood abounds. The wines, cheeses, chocolates, and other accouterments of wine culture are beautifully displayed.

Our wine-tasting professional, Kevin, was a shipping coordinator for Stone Hill. He talked a good wine talk, pushing vertical dinners and wine clubs. From him, I learned a new term, *wine library*. This is where good wines go when the producers decide to hide a few bottles from a good run and pretend they ran out. They age for a few years, appear at vertical dinners, then go on the shelves of the library for discerning patrons to request. There might be some choice Nortons in the Stone Hill library, he suggested.

From Kevin, I also learned that a lot of wines that are marketed as "fruit," such as blackberry wine, are mostly just grape wine with flavoring. I mean, sure, the main thing is to market a good product that people will buy, but it seems a little like cheating. Wine can actually be made with blackberries or blueberries or apples. Why not just make it that way?

The Stone Hill Nortons are delicious, but heavy on the oak. Kevin made the same joke about chewing on bark, but in this context, it was meant as a compliment to the wine. It's as if, between them, Stone Hill and Adam Puchta have agreed to cover the full taste spectrum of which Norton is capable, from fruity to woody.

Stone Hill makes an affordable Norton blend called the Ozark Hellbender, which Stone Hill Winery owner Nathan Held described as the winery's "top-selling red blend." This wine is named after the Ozark hellbender, a salamander that is marked endangered under the Endangered Species Act. Stone Hill collaborates with the St. Louis Zoo on the preservation of this noble reptile. To that end, a portion of the profits from Stone Hill's Hellbender wine go to save this environmentally critical amphibian.

The Ozark hellbender exists only in southern Missouri and a section of nearby Arkansas. It's a sedentary animal that mostly hides under rocks for its thirty years of life, going out at night to hunt small fish, especially crayfish. It leaves the shelter of its rocks during the day only when desperate to find a mate. My love of animals has me connecting emotionally with the shy, reclusive hellbender, even though I have never seen one. Why not hide under rocks all the time? The world is a cruel place. Destruction of the hellbender's habitat, especially a series of dams built in the 1940s and '50s, is one of the reasons that the hellbender population is in decline. Water contamination and speedboats are another two causes. We didn't need an actual bottle of wine after the wine tasting, but I bought a bottle of the Hellbender anyway and sat in a beautiful indoor patio with a skylight, part of Stone Hill's retail space.

A passion for saving Missouri wildlife is consistent with Stone Hill Winery owner Nathan Held's values generally. In an email interview, he mentions the importance of sustainability and resilience in the face of climate change. The winemaking industry will have to make "shifts to more sustainable and intentional farming management," he notes.[7]

Norton will play an important part in those accommodations, he believes: "Its future is bright as a wine grape due to its natural resistances to diseases and pests which are becoming more common, its ability to withstand changing climates, and its ability to produce delicious wines reminiscent and equal to wines from the greatest wine regions of the world."

Held is gratifyingly bullish on Norton: "Our Norton varietal is our flagship wine and continues to be one of our top sellers. Our varietal Norton wine brings us interest from consumers across the world who are curious to try a uniquely American wine and enjoy a relic of America's wine past and its bright future," he says.

I was somewhat surprised to learn that Held thinks Norton and Cynthiana may not be the same grape. "I have long held that they are distinct grapes, as the Pre-Prohibition wine and grape experts all found them to be quite similar but still distinct. Their descriptions make it quite clear that there were phenological and morphological differences," he says.

Like Parker Puchta, Held believes that wineries can make it on wine sales, if they have to. But "intentionally building experiences catered to creating memories for your customers allows for a healthier brand and company," he notes. In other words, the future of Missouri wine, Norton foregrounded, is somewhat dependent on tourism, but more dependent on making good wine.

Held is the third generation of Helds to own Stone Hill since it reopened in 1965. He is justly proud of his vineyard and winery, noting that it has existed longer than the wine industry in Napa Valley. From the 1890s to Prohibition, it was the nation's second-largest winery. Stone Hill was the first Missouri winery to reopen after Prohibition.

Though the wines disappeared, the stone building, erected by Michael Poeschel, which was the centerpiece of Stone Hill operations, somehow survived down the decades. A visitor to Stone Hill today might think the wine had always flowed. But bringing this winery back to life was a huge labor that involved not just love, but the vigilance of Sherlock Holmes.

In 1965, Jim Held bought what remained of the Stone Hill Winery with the promise to restore its historic legacy. He had grown up in a home winemaking family. He and his wife, Betty Ann Held, had some limited vineyard experience, having grown Catawba in nearby Pershing, Missouri.[8] However, no one had made Norton wine in Missouri since Prohibition.

If there is such a thing as destiny, the Helds appear to have it. Jim traced his ancestry back to 1837 and the first German immigrants to Missouri. He understood that the loss of the Norton grapes was the loss of an important artifact. It was a bit like losing track of the *Mona Lisa*. And finding it would be a treasure hunting score unlike any other.

He got a tip that a bootlegger, Paul Rauch, might have some Norton growing on his half acre, so Held made the ten-mile trek to Gasconade, Missouri, and combed Rauch's field, hunting the grape that could restore Stone Hill to its former majesty. There he found what he was looking for: the telltale, wide butterfly-shaped leaf, the tight bunch of almost black grapes. They had been there since before the Civil War. This was the fruit that Missouri would proudly declare its state grape when Norton wine was restored. It was a nearly wild grape on which Held would rebuild an industry. Held started growing Norton as soon as the weather permitted, with the help of his seven-year-old son, Jon, one of Jim and Betty Ann's four children. But he did not wait for those grapes to start making his legacy wine. He bought grapes directly from Rauch and bottled his first Norton.

The Helds' new enterprise was badly underfunded, and the family's first Norton had to be pressed with an old cider mill, Jon taking turns cranking it. Over the next decades, Norton wine from Stone Hill would win Missouri Wine Competition's triple crown for Best of Class Dry Red, Best Norton, and Best Overall in 2013, 2014, and 2017.

But the Helds' first Norton was not a success, Jim recounts in an interview with Todd Kliman.[9] He made an initial batch of fifteen thousand gallons and wished he had only made fifteen. The product had been bootstrapped by Jim, Betty Ann, their children, and some less-than-sterling employees. It was marketable—barely. Jim sold it. But it did not live up to his expectations of Norton or his expectations of himself. He did not yet know enough to produce the kind of wine he could take pride in. In the mid-1970s, Held went to California to study viticulture at the University of California. But Stone Hill's real success would germinate when Jon went to Cal State, Fresno, to get a degree in oenology.

Money is not the only kind of generational wealth to be passed down. Sometimes a passion is better than an estate. The Helds had not been wealthy when they purchased Stone Hill. They had been able to do so because Bill Harrison, who sold it, had a particular buyer in mind—someone who would ideally resurrect Missouri's great wine legacy. By the time Jon was of age, the Helds were still not a wealthy family. They sold wine and kept their business afloat. What Jim bestowed on Jon was not wealth; it was something better: a vision.

Jon was not a typical college student. He had a laser-like focus on his goal, the likes of which have mostly vanished from state universities. Every class, every field trip to a vineyard, was about what he could use to make wine in Missouri. He never made time for a football game. Anything less than an A in a class was unacceptable. He graduated with a 4.0 grade average. Even his girlfriend remarked that she would never be able to compete with his passion to put Stone Hill on the map.[10]

For fun, Jon played a game he invented that could be called "Identify That Wine." Having arrived on campus with bottles of his family's vintage, he would pour some into glasses and ask his friends to identify the varietal. They failed to do so, of course. They had never heard of Norton. It was a marketing opportunity, though, a way to get the name of Norton out there. This was not a trivial wine, Jon explained. It was serious.

He was not the only one of Jim and Betty Ann's children who would dedicate an education to wine. His younger sister, Patty, would follow in Jon's footsteps. His brother, Thomas, studied wine at the University of Arkansas and became a full-time wine researcher.

While Jon was in college, a promising vintner joined the Stone Hill team. This was Dave Johnson, a recent graduate of Michigan State's wine program. Johnson religiously read up on Hermann winemaking and discovered two important techniques that the Helds had been neglecting. To make a great Norton, the grapes needed to be left on the vine, and left some more, until they were actually turning to wine. This on-vine fermentation had been a trick of the Hermann Norton makers prior to Prohibition. The other important ingredient that had been lost were oak barrels in which to age the juice.

Finally, the newly arisen Stone Hill had a good young Norton. And, with a good wine comes the opportunity, some might say the obligation, to make a great wine that has been aged. This was the next step for the Helds, and it was a risk. To wait five to ten years for a wine is to play a long game, one that might or might not pay off. But it did pay off. The aged Norton got great reviews. Wine historian Paul Lukacs compared the mature product to the wines of the Rhône Valley in France, noting that age calms the fruit taste of a Norton, "and the wines develop earthy, even meaty secondary flavors."[11]

In 1993, wine critic Gerald Asher visited Missouri. By that time, Stone Hill had added a restaurant called Vintage 1847 in specific honor of the Norton grape's arrival in Missouri. Vintage specialized in gamey entrées like badger, possum, and raccoon. Asher wrote, amusingly, that he had a limited appetite for wildlife. He did, however, enjoy a venison steak with Norton red sauce in the company of Jon Held. The venison could not have been much fresher. That deer had been munching on some 1868 Norton grapes when it met its end, cheeky bugger.[12]

In his 1996 book, *Vineyard Tales*, Asher writes that the Norton is "an indigenous American grape that might yet do for Missouri what Cabernet Sauvignon has done for California."[13] Todd Kliman more or less re-created Asher's historic dinner at Stone Hill's Vintage 1847 around 2010 when he, too, dined there with Jon Held. Joel and I attempted to re-create the Vintage 1847 Gerald Asher–Jon Held–Todd Kliman dinners that resulted in so much good publicity for Norton wines. Somehow, I expected the restaurant itself to be bigger and grander. That's the effect of good writing.

In their writings about Stone Hill, Asher and Kliman make the winery's adjacent restaurant seem like the stuff of legends. And it has the gorgeous woodwork and high ceilings that are typical of Germanic Hermann. But without the wit of a Held, Asher, or Kliman, it was just a very nice restaurant.

As of 2023, the menu is substantially less risky. Mostly, it features the kind of red meats you could find at Kroger, no bear, moose, or freshly executed deer criminals. Green salads are in evidence, as is fish. There is even a vegetarian spaetzle on the menu. For a brief moment, I mourned the passing of the Asher era and foods that you would eat only on a dare. But then I breathed a longer sigh of relief for all the arteries and atrial valves that have been spared.

Joel was wined out and wanted a beer. I ordered a glass of Hellbender, which did as promised and paired beautifully with my cream of cabbage and sausage soup. Our high-backed wood booth was easily big enough to seat six people, but I was glad for its semiprivacy when I raised the soup bowl to my face to get the last sips out of the bottom. Most of the other patrons were quiet elderly couples, much like ourselves.

For dessert, I got a glass of pink Catawba, because hope so often triumphs over experience. I had yet to like a Catawba. The foxy sweetness is just off-putting enough to make me dread it. Unfortunately, this one was no exception. As much as I want to love all American wines, the Catawba tasted like Kool-Aid, but with the substantial virtue of being alcoholic. It was a beautiful color. I took a beat and reminded myself that I am a lover, not a critic. Someone craves Catawba as much as I crave Norton, and neither of us is wrong.

The Horton Norton

We must backtrack in time to 1988 when Dennis Horton, a native of Hermann, requisitioned a shipment of Norton vines from Stone Hill and planted them at his new winery in Virginia. The Norton vines had returned home after over a hundred years. They would be an important brick in building Virginia's current wine industry.

As a child, Horton had played in what he regarded as the "catacombs." This playground was actually Stone Hill's historic wine cellar, built by Michael Poeschel. Those cellars were a perfect hideaway for boys, a place away from the adults, a mysterious canvas onto which one could project boyhood fantasies, and they smelled of mushrooms.

Only as a young adult did Horton learn that this cellar was a critical component of Missouri's economic narrative. When Horton was a student at the University of Missouri, Columbia, Jim Held took possession of Stone Hill and started the process of converting it back into a winery. Those cellars, it turned out, held more mystery than Horton had understood as a child.

He had grown up only a block away from the mushroom farm. He was a typical Hermann youth who knew nothing about the former grandeur of Hermann's wine culture. He had been taught nothing about that glorious past. Hermann's august history had been largely lost. Anyone who knew of it rarely spoke of it.

He became a serious wine drinker while serving in the U.S. Air Force, stationed in Ipswich, England. The English food was deplorable, but discovering good French wines to wash it down with was a whole new adventure. Before returning to the United States, Horton visited France and Germany, where he tasted wines in earnest, making notes, learning the names of things. He served in the military for three and a half years, and that was more than enough. He had only joined the Air Force to avoid the worst consequences of being drafted. At the University of Maryland, College Park, he earned a marketing degree, married a woman named Sharon, and immediately displayed a strong knack for business. He increased profitability at two office supply businesses before starting up his own company.

By the late 1970s, he was wealthy enough to pursue almost any dream. And his mind kept going back to wine. He read widely about grape growing and viticulture, about soil, climate, chemistry. At his home in Aroda, a two-hour drive from Washington DC, he started up a small vineyard and cared for it meticulously.

He was no longer a child, playing in wine cellars, unaware of the amazing history attached to them. He knew the history of Hermann and how it was tied to the Norton grape. He knew of Norton's origins in Virginia, his adoptive state, and he knew of its resurrections in his hometown of Hermann. From that history, he also knew that the Norton could be grown, bottled, and sold within five years. It did not require decades of growing and aging to make a decent wine. Horton, now in his middle years, would have time to make Norton wine from scratch.

Furthermore, it astounded Horton that no one had seriously considered bringing Norton back to Virginia as the German Americans were busily doing in Missouri. Kliman writes, "It boggled his mind that, aside from a handful of small, experimental plantings . . . nobody had thought to bring the Norton all the way back, to restore the pride and glory of antebellum Virginia's vineyards to the cradle."[14]

It now seems inevitable that Norton wine would return to Virginia, where it had been born, discovered, celebrated as the one grape that could survive the Virginia soil and weather and still make a dry wine. If Horton had not brought it back, would someone else have risen to the challenge? Or would Virginia's winemakers still be making inferior versions of French wines like Pinot Noir and Cabernet, as they were in 1989, when Horton established his first commercial vineyard?

Horton bought a small area of farmland in Gordonsville, Virginia, which was the start of Horton Vineyards. His wife, Sharon, became the vineyard manager. It was located near enough to his offices that he hoped not to exhaust himself running two very different businesses. Horton Vineyards was not the first vineyard in post-Prohibition Virginia, but it was one of only forty. Due to advances in winemaking technology, *vinifera* vines could now be grown in Virginia, and they were being grown. It was a fear-based decision for most grape growers. The snobbery that excludes any local or unfamiliar wine out of so many stores made it safer to bottle poor copies of California's wines, themselves clones of French vintages.

As most vineyard owners do, Horton lost money for four years before starting to turn a profit. His Viognier was the first wine to bring in the awards and recognition, earning ninety-one points from Robert Parker. As a direct result of Horton's success with Viognier, it became Virginia's state grape.

Horton's first efforts were experimental. His research showed that Cabernet Franc would do well in soil that would not produce a decent Cabernet Sauvignon. "I'll always love him for bringing Cabernet Franc to Virginia," says vineyard consultant Lucie Morton.[15]

Norton was, perhaps, his inspiration, but his Viognier was indisputably his most beloved wine, made from a white grape with less acidity than Sauvignon Blanc. Fermented properly, it can produce a fuller-bodied wine than the Blanc.

Viognier has been exported from the French Rhône Valley to Australia, New Zealand, Israel, North and South America, and Africa. Horton developed an interest in the grape while in France and from reading the work of wine writer Jancis Robinson.

The 2018 obituaries of Horton report that he also grew Rkatsiteli, Tannat, Syrah, Touriga, Marsanne, Roussanne, Nebbiolo, and Pinotage, producing wines that could be replicated by other Virginia wine growers. During his lifetime, the number of wineries in Virginia grew from 40 to approximately 280.[16] Wine technician Brad McCarthy makes huge claims for Horton's influence on the resurgence of Norton winemaking: "There are whole wineries based on growing Norton now, thanks to Dennis Horton."[17] Alan Kinne, an early winemaker for Horton Vineyards, says, "It was Dennis who completely woke up the slumbering Virginia wine industry by believing that varieties other than chardonnay and cabernet sauvignon would make Virginia a viable entity."[18]

Horton liked to joke that he would rather be lucky than smart, but in reality, he had to be both. To an outside observer, it might seem that Horton had more than his fair share of luck. But his success was backed by sacrifice and perfectionism as well. "I've ripped out more vines than most people in this state have ever planted," he told the *Washington Post*. That pursuit of perfection followed him into the laboratory. Kinne reports spending days tweaking the nuances of a new wine before Horton declared it a winner.[19]

Paul Roberts

In the mid-1990s, Paul Roberts and his wife, Nadine Grabania, dipped a toe in the winemaking business by planting a half acre of Cynthiana in Pennsylvania. Starting up a vineyard had been a lifelong dream for Roberts. He had cherished that dream since interning at Chateau Montelena in Napa Valley, California. Chateau Montelena is most famous as the winery that shook the wine industry to its foundations by winning a blind competition with French wines in the famed Judgment of Paris.

Starting out, Paul and Nadine experimented with the Cynthiana/Norton grape, encountering the usual and unusual obstacles that confront new vineyards. One year, wildlife decimated their crop, devouring nearly every single grape. Roberts documents his setbacks and eventual success in his autobiographical book, *From This Hill, My Hand, Cynthiana Wine*. The couple moved their business to Maryland, where they fought and won a seven-year campaign to outlaw fracking in the state. In 2017, Maryland became a frack-free zone, an unusual victory in a nation in love with cheap, easy energy.

When I caught up with Roberts by phone, he and his wife had stopped growing grapes. Instead, they specialize in making wines from grapes grown by nearby farmers. Their winery, Deep Creek Cellars, makes Pinot Grigio, Pinot Blanc, and a variety of red blends that bring together Cabernet Franc, Chambourcin, and other ingredients.

Roberts cites climate change and the "extremely bizarre" spring weather in western Maryland as the reason he and Nadine decided to tear up their grapevines.[20] "Late frosts are a problem," Roberts says. It used to be the case that growers could depend on a frost-free spring starting May 1. That's no longer a reliable milestone, however. Starting in 2010, he says, the grape-growing season started on March 15. The weather is simply too unpredictable for wine grape growing, Roberts concludes. Two winters were so harsh, it killed their rootstock, and they had to start over. The next year brought the seventeen-year locusts. "It was never a really successful enterprise. I'd love to grow grapes. Financially, we couldn't keep taking those kinds of body blows," Roberts says.

In the war between Roberts and nature, "nature came out ahead," he gently quips. His winery still makes a Norton. Ursa Major, a Deep Creek Cellars wine with a black bear on the bottle, is made from 100 percent Norton grapes. Roberts thinks that Norton is an important varietal because of its potential to be grown organically. It's a potential that goes largely unexploited, though. Most Norton growers do rely on spraying, though Roberts points out that he never sprayed his own Cynthiana. And it flourished. Roberts also praises the Norton/Cynthiana's ability to grow in a wide variety of soils and climates. "To my knowledge, there is no other wine varietal that will grow in both Texas and Iowa," he notes.

Jennifer McCloud

Horton passed a number of torches, one, you might say, for every new grape he introduced to Virginia. But I am chasing Cynthiana, so the torch I am most interested in is the one he passed to Jennifer McCloud. Jenni, as she introduces herself, became the next champion of Norton grapes and wine in the 1990s. And she holds that title today.

Something we Norton drinkers have in common is a come-to-Jesus moment. We remember the first time we tasted, then guzzled, a Cynthiana/Norton. "It blew my mind," McCloud tells the *Washington Post*.[21] As it was with me, so with Paul, and so with Jenni. There was no walking back that moment.

The year her mind was blown was 1995, when she first attended an American Society of Enology and Viticulture meeting. There, she discovered not only the Norton but also its chief advocates: Horton and Kinne. Horton would pass not only the torch of his Norton enthusiasm but also his winemaker.

Kinne went to work for McCloud's newly established Chrysalis Winery. Under her close eye, the cocoon of Norton's potential would unfold and find its audience. "It has this incredible intensity and extraction that allows it to hold its fruit while it ages to a graceful and beautiful bouquet, on par with the other great red wines of the world," she tells Wine Enthusiast in 2022.[22]

Like Horton, McCloud had made her fortune in something else before turning her imagination to wine. Until she tasted the Norton, she had flirted with the idea of growing grapes and making wine in Oregon. The Norton changed all that. Only the Norton's native state of Virginia would do. She planted six acres of Norton in 1998; now she has forty acres dedicated to that grape.[23] Kinne's advice was to make a wine you like to drink. Well, that was definitely the Norton. As he had advised Horton, he also advised McCloud to plant Petit Menseng, though it was admittedly a long shot. McCloud also planted Fer Servadou and Albarino, as well as the state's highly successful Viognier.[24]

Like other Norton fans, McCloud was inspired by the Norton's distinct taste as well as by its historicity, its importance in the tapestry of American history. That does not mean that she neglects the technical aspects of winemaking. In her vineyard, the Norton vines are trained on their trellises so that the fruit lies on top of the leaves, rather than underneath the leaves as grapes grow naturally. This keeps the fruit dryer and less susceptible to mildew and rot, the everlasting enemies of winemakers, especially in Virginia's very humid growing season. From their position above the leaves, the grapes get better sun and an occasional breeze.

By the time the *Washington Post* profiled her in 2009, McCloud had copyrighted the slogan "Norton, the Real American Grape!"[25] Despite its undisputable content of *vinifera,* McCloud refers to Norton as a "native plant," pointing to its hardiness, especially its disease resistance, a quality generally shared by plants that are original to the region where they are grown.

The year 2009 also found McCloud moving purposely among her vines, followed by up to thirty rescue dogs and receiving acknowledgment for two Norton-based wines, the Norton Locksley Reserve and Sara's Patio Red, which, despite its ambiguous name, is 100 percent Norton.[26] Tongue in cheek, she enjoyed poking a little fun at Zinfandel. To *Post* staff writer Catherine Cheney, McCloud floats the idea of a Norton advocates group titled Norton Advocates and Producers, NAP for short. NAP is a play on ZAP, which stands for Zinfandel Advocates and Producers. "Is zinfandel putting you to sleep? Try Norton," she quips.[27] By 2022, Wine Enthusiast reported that she was making six thousand cases of Norton a year and also exporting grapes to ten other wineries.

In a 2023 phone interview, McCloud remains fully bullish about Norton. But it will always be a divisive wine, she indicates: "Some people just don't find it an attractive alcoholic beverage, and other people fall in love with it." She talks about how well Norton ages. Where Cabernet Sauvignon starts its bottled life at noon, Norton starts at 8 a.m. So, the Norton can afford a long aging period. "Being a different species allows for a graceful and very long aging profile. Old Nortons are just fantastic," she says. Norton ages just as beautifully as Rhône and Nebbiolo, she indicates: "Over time, the fruitiness attenuates, and the bottle bouquet develops."[28]

McCloud has interesting advice for young wine investors. Buy wine varietals that age well; lay them down properly, somewhere that has a consistently cool temperature (not the basement!); and let time make them more valuable. And, if you want to grow Norton grapes, McCloud and her staff are growing them for sale. She has devised a growing system that accommodates the Norton grape's fussiness about being propagated. When she first started growing Norton in her nursery, the plants would take root, then bud beautifully. But they would then die within a matter of weeks. The solution? "We have a heated greenhouse, where we heat the root zone, and cool the top. It's a little slower to grow," McCloud explains, but the growth is surer.[29]

In the time I've been writing this book, I've visited three Kentucky wineries that serve Norton, and all were within easy driving distance of my home in Louisville. Even my cabin in north Georgia is within an hour and a half of at least two wineries making Cynthiana. So I have to ask Jenni: Is she the reason that so many regions are now growing and bottling Norton? "We've had a hand in that, but so have a lot of others," she replies modestly. McCloud likes to point out that, when Americans grow European wines, they're effectively copying something, and those copies will never be as good. "Virginia is never going to out-California California. But Virginia wines are more elegant, less obvious and arguably better with food. In a world where many wines speak of sameness, Virginia speaks of a region," McCloud tells Wine Enthusiast.[30]

This pride of place is a big reason that McCloud threw so much of her reputation behind Norton. She didn't want to produce wines that would inevitably get compared to European wines. She never wanted to hear the words "For a Virginia Merlot, that's pretty good."[31] The phrase "Cabernet is king" has long governed American winemakers and growers, encouraging them to fall back on what is known to work, even if it's a little too safe. Does growing Cabernet and other European vintages suggest a lack of imagination? Maybe, McCloud thinks: "I'm a boomer, and I think that people that are going to start a winery—these are folks that see the prestige and glory of owning a winery, but they're mostly drinking scotch. They're not that much into wines. They gravitate to that which they do know."[32]

"'We're going to grow Cabernet Franc,' they say. You can make some good Cabernet Franc in Virginia. But, no matter how good we make a Cabernet, the standard is still over there," she adds.[33] It should be noted that Norton is but one wine in the constellation of wines that Chrysalis produces. McCloud is also very involved in Albarino viticulture. And Chrysalis produces Nebbiolo, Viognier, and the intriguingly named Snobby Bitch White Sangria (which I must now try, if only because of the name), among others.

McCloud's strongest contempt is reserved for the people who only grow or drink the most obvious French varietals. "You sorry person, you are missing out on a wealth of interesting wine," she says. Some new vineyard owners, she notes, "have a false sense of the luxury aspect of having a winery, but they're not really into the plants." By contrast, McCloud identifies strongly as a farmer. Her outgoing phone message says "Welcome to the ag district." She notes that growing grapes and making wine is but one of her businesses. She also owns a dairy that makes craft cheeses and a bakery.[34]

All this takes place in Loudoun County, which George Washington once called the "breadbasket of the American Revolution." I asked McCloud the same question I've been asking other winemakers: We know Norton/Cynthiana has a strong following, but who are these people? McCloud says to imagine a bell curve. At the beginning of the curve are the brand-new wine drinkers, the Cabernet-only wine enthusiasts. Past that are the newcomers with a little more wine knowledge, and they are the ones most likely to embrace Norton because they haven't been overly coached about what they're supposed to like.[35]

But that's only one of Norton's followings. Past the bell curve hump, in what McCloud describes as the "long tail," are the truly knowledgeable and experienced wine drinkers, and a percentage of Norton drinkers are in this part of the curve. These are "experienced wine drinkers that have been around the block if not the world," she says.[36]

McCloud agrees with me that the wine industry is still beset with snobbery. But she believes that the upcoming generation of wine drinkers will change all that. "The new generation has the 'this is not your father's oldsmobile' attitude. They arrive at their own likes and dislikes," she says. At the same time, McCloud thinks that, when people fall back on the same traditional wines, it's mostly out of insecurity: "Part of the problem is the lack of education and a personal insecurity about wines." But what wine enthusiasts need to understand is that "there's no one who knows everything about wine. It is so diverse, so many grape varieties, so many it's fucking intimidating," she adds.[37]

The National Museum of American History dedicated an exhibit titled "Return of the Native" to the Norton grape and wine in which McCloud figured impressively. She donated a grape-picking basket that her pickers wear, which is modeled on traditional Virginia apple-picking gear. The basket, which attaches to the front of the picker, allows that worker to work with both hands and reduces the bending that injures such workers. The exhibit also featured a razor knife, donated by McCloud, that Chrysalis employees use to cut the tough stems of the Norton.

Fig. 1. Exterior of the Baker-Bird Winery.

Fig. 2. George Bayer, founder of Hermann, Missouri.

Fig. 3. The Grape Expectations bed-and-breakfast plays on Hermann's wine tourism and history.

Fig. 4. A 2018 reserve Norton at Adam Puchta Winery.

Fig. 5. Exterior of Chateau Aux Arc.

Fig. 6. Chateau Aux Arc sold quite a few Cynthiana vines during the COVID pandemic.

Fig. 7. A glass of Niagara at Wiederkehr Restaurant.

Fig. 8. Savant, a blend of Catawba and Norton.

Fig. 9. A road sign for the Post Winery in Altus, Arkansas.

Fig. 10. Muscadine juice at the Post Winery.

5
The Cult of Cynthiana

As a child, I crisscrossed the country with my itinerant mother. She had to be a college professor, and hope sprang eternal that she would find a secure position in the misogynistic realm of evangelical education. By the time she had finally found a permanent job, in her late fifties, my childhood had been spent relocating from Chicago to rural South Carolina to Denver to Germany to Spain, back to Denver, then on to Philadelphia, then back to Chicago. Every Christian college she taught at exploited her vulnerability. She would arrive in a new state with the promise of a single income and no social network, the challenge of establishing a new home in rental accommodations and navigating a brand-new set of politics at a new job.

The best thing about my childhood might have been the road trips between her jobs. These were rare intervals when my mother wasn't looking over her shoulder and worrying about whether the impression she was making was acceptably demure and virtuous. We had good days on the road when she could just be herself. We frequently stopped at roadside attractions, museums, and monuments. Her quirky observations about these things were a joy for me. I was desperate for souvenirs so that I could retain the memory of these moments.

I begged for postcards and picked up useless trinkets from cheap hotels—coasters, stationery, brochures, maps—and paper placemats from chain restaurants. But these mementos invariably got chucked when it was time to move again. We couldn't afford professional movers, so if it didn't fit in the car, it went in the dumpster. My attempt to keep fetishes in my life annoyed her.

This is all to say that, when I crossed over into Arkansas, in my ten-year-old hybrid Camry, I didn't know if it was my first time in that state. I have a nagging memory of a postcard, but no memories of Arkansas itself. It seemed incumbent to make this pilgrimage to Altus, Arkansas, where several wineries uphold the tradition of making Cynthiana. I had no particular expectations except that it would be hot, at least nominally southern, and verdant. I was not wrong about any of that.

Especially the heat. It was the end of July, and Altus is at the foot of the Ozarks. I didn't expect that to provide any relief, and it didn't. Nor did the abundant, reckless greenery, which was everywhere off the interstate, layered with weeds growing over weeds, an excess of vitality, like a baroque concerto.

The trip from my home in Blue Ridge, Georgia, took two days. I stopped for food only twice, both times at a Waffle House. Not that I'm a huge fan of Waffle House. But it's amazing how Waffle House rockets to the top of the list when the other options are McDonalds, Hardees, Sonic, and a closed Pizza Hut. "Did you find a vegetable?" Joel quipped during one of our phone calls. He knew full well that the answer would be, "Well, there were some sliced pickles." There were also some beans in my chili. One must be grateful for small blessings.

Signs for the Post Winery appear on the highway leading into Ozark, Arkansas, and I was too early to check in to my Airbnb, so I took the exit. Immediately, I was in the real Arkansas. Real in the sense that little has changed in the past hundred years or so. The greenery was magnificent. I have never been to a jungle, and it seemed that no place could be more alive, or the forces of nature more strong. The road that leads to several wineries on St. Mary's Mountain is badly in need of repair, but that adds to the strong sense of going back in time or at least getting away from urban sprawl.

We know, from numerous texts published in the 1800s and lovingly curated by Google Books, that Cynthiana wine and Cynthiana grapes are mentioned alongside Norton, going back to the first mentions of either. And most people accept that they are the same grape. But Arkansas does not provide the kind of richly embroidered origin story for Cynthiana that Missouri and Virginia have for Norton. I scoured dozens of resources, and what they agreed was that Cynthiana was found in the woods.

I was hoping for a narrative similar to that of the newly widowed Daniel Norton fiercely fighting for a grape that probably grew wild on his farm. But the lack of such a story, the insistence that Cynthiana is just a wild grape, native to Arkansas, actually makes it even more exciting to people who think you should love native plants and eat locally grown fruits and vegetables. The fact that the scientists couldn't find any real differences between Norton and Cynthiana just proves that it's a native grape, growing in various places all over North America, oblivious to the need for a better origin story.

My first Arkansas winery was Chateau Aux Arc. Pulling into the drive there was like stumbling upon a wealthy French farm. The landscaping and plantings were all carefully chosen and attended to. Several tall trees cast enough shade to allow patrons to sit on benches even in the midday heat and enjoy the outdoors. I was wondering why anyone would give an Arkansas winery a French name; the pretension seemed to come out of nowhere. But my Airbnb host set me straight. "Aux Arc" is actually the name of a nearby bend in the Arkansas River, so named by the French explorers who believed themselves to be discovering it. The Quapaw Indians, in fact, had been around, naming things themselves for quite some time.

The "arc" in the river bend is analogous to the Paris landmark called the Arch of Triumph. More amazingly, "aux arc" sounds like "Oh, Arc!" And that's where the Ozark Mountains and region got its American-sounding name. The sound of "arc" also features in the state name, but that has its origins elsewhere.

A hand-painted sign under a tall tree advises people that they can buy Cynthiana vines for fifteen dollars each. It will turn out that the winery is back-ordered by three years on this offer. A lot of people decided to grow grapes during the two-year COVID-19 scare. So the winery has had to hit the pause button on selling vines. Since it takes three years to grow a grapevine to the point of productivity, three years out seemed like a good enough place to stop sales, according to the woman who conducted my tasting.

Audrey House owns Chateau Aux Arc, and the winery's website boasts that she is the first and only female wine grower in Arkansas.[1] Like other winemakers who don't inherit a business, she fell in love with viticulture through a side door. While studying psychology at the University of Oklahoma in

Norman, she worked at the university's greenhouse. There, her green thumb surfaced, and she found her destiny as a grower.

In 1998, she bought twenty acres of neglected farmland, ten acres of which were Chardonnay vines planted in 1980, from one of the Al Wiederkehrs who are the patriarchs of wine in the Arkansas Ozarks. (More on the Wiederkehren later.) She lived in a tent for a year and recruited friends and visitors to help her with her vines. By the age of thirty-three, she was a master sommelier and featured in Arkansas Business's "40 under 40" issue.

It is impossible not to be impressed with Audrey House. Not just because she is a solo woman entrepreneur and a scrappy bootstrapper, but also because she fought for shipping rights before the Arkansas Legislature in 2017. Shipping rights, I am learning, are integral to the survival of all U.S. wineries and vineyards. Prior to the recently improved legislation, it was difficult for Arkansas wineries to ship even to customers within their own state, according to the Chateau Aux Arc website.[2]

It was House who, in 2009, worked with state leaders to have Cynthiana named Arkansas's state grape. Is it fudging a little, when Norton is the state grape of Missouri, and it's the same grape, according to scientists? No, it is not. Turns out two states can have the same symbol. Thirty-two of our states have state birds that are state birds in other states. Who knew?

In any event, House has the proud distinction of being a legislative gadfly, to the point where, around the state capitol, she has the name "grape lady." For eight years in the twenty-first century's second decade, House was the Alternative Energy Commissioner, under Governors Mike Beebe and Asa Hutchinson. Perhaps the most thrilling statement on the Chateau Aux Arc website is this one: "We already know Arkansas wine is just as good as Napa."[3]

House didn't return my call, but the woman who administered my tasting said she was the winery owner's best friend. More than anything, I am dying to get a sense of who is drinking Cynthiana. Because Parker Puchta in Missouri reported many sales of Norton to Chicago, I asked about that at the Chateau. House's best friend said she does most of the shipping, and that most of her customers buy directly from the winery. No, they do not sell a lot to Chicago, but they do sell heavily to Texas, she reported.

My imagination wanders again, this time to a lavish ranch-style house, decorated in fifty shades of brown and beige with one of those chandeliers that features the graceful antlers of a dead animal. (It *must* have the chandelier. Please don't take this away from me.) Inside this Texan palace sits a lonely millionaire in rattlesnake boots and a ten-gallon hat, sipping on Cynthiana, hating the north, also hating Mexico, and dreaming of better days when all these wind turbine–pushing tree huggers weren't disrespecting oil. (The hat *must* be worn in the house. I have met very few Texans, but I cannot imagine one without a hat.)

The shipping coordinator tells me that a wine called Altage is their bestseller. According to the website, this varietal, packaged in a distinctive blue bottle, is a blend of Niagara, Stueben, Jupiter, and Vignoles. It is marketed as sweet and fruity, pretty much the opposite of what I am looking for. Before I can stop her, House's best friend pours me a plug of Zinfandel, which I now have to politely drink. I hear Joel's voice in my head, demanding to know "WHY?" Why are Americans still growing this? Still trying to compete with Europe on wines that were never that good to begin with?

The next bestseller, my tasting expert informs me, is the winery's Cynthiana. Though the website boasts several wines of this vintage, they are clean out. No Cynthiana Gold Cap, no Cynthiana Silver Cap, no intriguingly named Cynthiana Teal Reserve with a teal label.

My sommelier says that Chateau Aux Arc has the second-largest collection of Cynthiana, and I believe her, even though she hasn't specified whether she means second-largest in state, country, or world. This does not alter the fact that there is no Cynthiana at this winery. This will prove to be the theme of my Arkansas trip. It's gone, and no, we can't or won't tell you who is drinking it all.

My trip to Arkansas was both well and poorly timed. Well timed because I was there in time for the grape festival. Poorly because I was there the week before harvest. A few months after harvest, I have to presume, is when one might actually score some Cynthiana. Or perhaps one needs to be a club member. The day was not lost, though. Someone at Chateau Aux Arc has a sense of humor because their club is named the Wineaux Club, a group of winos with pretensions. So I got a chuckle out of that.

When I revealed that I was in Arkansas mostly to chase Cynthiana, my sommelier trotted out a bottle of Savant, a blend of Catawba and Cynthiana. My little mind is blown. It was so obvious! Catawba is too sweet, Cynthiana arguably too acidic, at least sometimes. Put them together; make them balance each other out! Brilliant! A wise move, hence the name Savant. It is, for my taste, quite a good wine. Only a little sweet, not cloying, good depth, mellow. It would pair well with any of the foods that Cynthiana is known to pair with. I left with a bottle of it.

Would the winery be making an appearance at the grape festival, I asked. No, my server said. She would be staying indoors where the temperature was a consistent seventy-two degrees. She expected to see quite a few festivalgoers. They would be driven there by the heat, she predicted: "They will be hot," and the winery would be offering sanctuary. It was indeed hot out the day I arrived in Altus and every subsequent day. I sought out a Walmart because it was clear that nothing in my suitcase would be light enough or scanty enough to deal with the outdoor heat, and most of the festival would be conducted outdoors. Traditions can be cruel like that.

I located a dress and a white halter top, both of which had in-built padding over the chest. This kind of lining has become absolutely necessary because a bra feels like a lead vest in any heat over eighty-seven degrees. I have simply reached the point of being unable to tolerate a bra in summer. And yet the sight of nipples can be misconstrued, even in a married woman with large dogs and a huge, hairy husband.

The halter top and dress are wildly inappropriate for a woman of my age, education, sense of irony, comportment . . . well, shit, who *can* wear ruffles, prints, and strings? Everything in Walmart looks like it was made for an off-duty high school cheerleader. What would be appropriate for a woman like me would be either a burka or a three-piece suit, but I wouldn't survive two minutes outside in that.

New clothes in hand, I calculate the amount of time it will take to recross the parking lot and get back to my car, take a deep breath, and charge out the automatic door, forgetting that the car will have heated up during the twenty minutes I was shopping.

Around this point, Joel called to tell me that air conditioning systems were designed to cool houses down by all of twenty degrees and that, with temperatures of 110, people are miserable in their homes, even with the air cranked up to full capacity. A random google search on the words "people with air conditioning die of heat anyway" turns up a *Time Magazine* article titled, depressingly enough, "Air Conditioning Will Not Save Us." And it was published a year ago. "Compared to other weather-related disasters, the emergency response to extreme heat from U.S. leaders has been minimal," the article avers.[4] Well, yes. All eyes were on COVID while this giant hovered in plain sight.

As the car is cooking me, I have a revelation about how the climate will kill humanity. Well, not all of us. The old and those with chronic illness will go first. Central air conditioning systems will fail, many babies will be unable to tolerate the heat, hospitals won't be able to accommodate everyone. They will die in parking lots and ambulances. It will be like COVID—sordid, but not dramatic. Most of the deaths will take place out of the public eye. Every year, the rising number of heat-related deaths will seem more normal, simply because it happened last year and the year before. Humans are the masters of self-desensitization.

The population will decline, but slowly, and newscasters will always put the best, most smiling spin on it. Sure, lots of people died last year, but science!, hope!, faith!, birth rates!, and so on. Over five hundred years, a new race of humans will have evolved to endure temperatures well over a hundred degrees. Millionaires will live in the Arctic and in the highest mountains. A sparse population of low-tech hunter-gatherers will roam the woods of Arkansas, Georgia, and Kentucky in loincloths. To keep the giant mosquitoes from flying up their butts. Much like *The Walking Dead*, but without the zombies.

My Airbnb turns out to be in an elegant neighborhood of sprawling meadow-like lawns and towering trees. It's not quite a plantation, but it has that flavor. It reminds me of those movies, like *The View from Pompey's Head*, in which a southern woman, lacking nothing, is nevertheless frustrated and unhappy in her giant house with her well-trained servants, her carefully engineered foundation garments, and her perfectly ironed linen shirts.

She squandered her chance at love, long ago. And we are supposed to feel sorry for her. I can never relate to these movies. How can you squander your chance at love? I have made many mistakes, but how can anyone make that one? Still, even if I had a house that size, I would have other worries, like how to pay for the air conditioning.

My host, Jelsomin ("Call me Jelsi"), has solved this problem by opening an Airbnb, which makes sense. She escorted me to a beautifully appointed room that was not yet ninety degrees but not cool either. She would turn on the air, she said. Eventually. I took that as my cue to take a long bath in cold water and leave my hair as wet as possible. Eleven minutes away is the Wiederkehr (pronounced Weed-icker, according to a local historian) Restaurant and wine cellar. The Wiederkehrs have lived and made wine in this neck of Arkansas for five generations. They have their own municipality, called Wiederkehr Village.

At first, I thought this was just marketing, but no. Wiederkehr has its own dot-gov website and a city council on which sit three Wiederkehrs, including Adam, the latest descendant and general manager. He manages two restaurants and the Wiederkehr WeinGarten, according to his LinkedIn profile.

Lunch at Wiederkehr Restaurant is elegant in a manner reminiscent of the 1960s. Tudor-style half-timbering prevails as the decor theme, along with dark and uncomfortable furniture. Strings of white Christmas lights mitigate the gloom. Lit candles stuck in wine bottles drip their many-colored waxes down the sides. There's a hybridization of fantasy Italian and fantasy Swiss that is kind of fascinating.

The waitstaff, all young women, wear traditional Swiss dresses, embroidered, with puffy sleeves, loose skirts, and lace-up bodices. I haven't seen this kind of outfit since 2009, and it was pretty cliché then. No doubt, though, there are people who love this style of restaurant and find comfort in going to one where these conventions are still practiced.

I ordered a glass of Cynthiana with my turkey sandwich. The waitress came back to my table to explain that they were "out of it." I couldn't tell whether she was talking about my food order or my wine order, but eventually, we worked out that they had no Cynthiana, for love or money, neither by glass nor by bottle.

It became obvious that my waitress and I were mutually annoyed with each other. To her, I'm a tedious old woman, taking up an entire table as a solo diner, inherently weird, and ordering things that are not in the kitchen. To me, she is yet another disappointing millennial, no empathy, poor communication skills, yet somehow smug in her lack of self-awareness.

Somehow, I have to stop her from reading the list of red wines to me. She is a slave to the script, like any good salesperson. I ordered a red wine; I must want red wine. I could try to explain that I don't want red wine, per se—I'm on a quest for native grapes, but this is doomed to make me even weirder, threatening the thin veneer of patience she has for me.

I ordered the blush Niagara. According to Wikipedia and all its touted neutrality, Niagara is not an "optimal" grape for winemaking. My experience with it bears that out. Up to that point, I had never had a memorable Niagara. Yet independent winemakers keep making wine from it. The Wiederkehr Niagara was surprisingly decent; it sported an approachable bouquet, pleasant enough taste and aftertaste. It paired surprisingly well with the turkey. Emboldened by the discovery of a decent Niagara, I felt brave enough to order a glass of dessert Concord wine. It seemed that the restaurant was proud of it, as they were charging more for this dessert than for the table wines. In fact, it was nasty. The foxiness of *Vitis labrusca* can be pleasant. Sometimes I think I am the only person in the universe who troubles to ferret out the pungent quality of it. But the fox on that wine was swampy.

I heard my mother's voice in my head, from childhood, reminding me that there are starving children in Africa. More compelling than the starving Africans, for me, as an id-driven child, were the stories of the Depression through which she lived as a child, the food shortages, the people coming to her door to beg for food, the pots of onions and potatoes kept on the stove because no one could be sent away empty-handed. These were the stories that made it impossible for me to waste food, even bad wine. But I prevailed over my upbringing and left it behind. Even more than I can't bear to waste food, I can't bear to take in calories that bring no pleasure.

I timed my Altus adventure to coincide with the annual grape festival, which takes place in the town's public park. The lineup included a good deal of live music, grape stomping, and vendors, but the heat was the main feature, as my sommelier at Chateau Aux Arc predicted. I need to quit being so apocalyptic about the heat. It's always hot in the summer. Some people handle it better than others. Obviously, I'm not one of "some people."

The festival took place on a Friday evening and all day Saturday. On Friday, there was only one actual winery represented at the festival, and that was Mount Bethel. There were the usual food trucks, along with the smell of dead and roasting animal flesh, with accompanying smoke. Many vendors were selling goods unrelated to grapes or wine. The usual T-shirt sales, dresses of original design, craftsmen. A bottle maker had spread some very beautiful wares on a table for this event but was getting little traffic.

The agenda promised a "media stomp." This turned out to be a fairly random collection of four people who took off their shoes and stepped into barrels to stomp a quantum of grapes. They drew a crowd, possibly because of the presence of one *very* pretty local media person who was quite dolled up to press grapes. It was obvious she was used to the spotlight and knew how to deal with it. She posed enthusiastically for many amateur photographers and at least one news camera.

The media stomp turned out to be a contest to see who could produce the most grape juice in a short burst of stomping. Careful pains were taken to make sure this was fairly conducted. Contestants started and stopped stomping at the same time under supervision. Then each bucket was poured and strained for exactly the same number of seconds. The resulting juice was then put into bottles, and the bottle with the most juice won. The bottles looked almost identically full to me, so I was glad I wasn't judging that.

As to the grape pie eating and racing with a grape in a spoon, I decided I could miss most of that. If the god I don't believe in intended us to eat grapes in pies, she wouldn't have invented wine. A lot of families attended, and it seemed to mostly be a local event at which people from Ozark and Altus could meet and chat. Very low-key.

Most of the festival action turned out to be in the wineries where the air conditioning was flowing alongside the wine. They were crowded, mostly with people over forty who had time on their hands. The servers at the bars and tastings, however, were mostly very young people. Some of them were obviously in training to be the next winemakers and sommeliers. Some, like the young woman who poured for me at Mount Bethel, were pressed into service on an annual basis. She is part of the family that owns the winery, and she was working alongside her two siblings and their aunt.

Mount Bethel makes a Cynthiana, but they had none available for tasting on that day. "We had a Cynthiana!" my server explained. She didn't know which, if any, of the wines were made with local grapes. The Vignoles was delicious. But the wine that really surprised me was the white Muscadine. It did not taste like a fruit drink rendered from powder and water, as the Muscadine wines of my past have tasted. It had some dimensions, some layering. Fruity as expected, but not bland or overwhelmingly sweet.

The scientific name for Muscadine is *Vitis rotundifolia*. Like *Vitis labrusca* and *Vitis aestivalis, rotundifolia* is a native American grape. The vines grow wild all over the southeastern United States, as far north as New Jersey and west all the way to Oklahoma. It needs only a little cultivation to grow big, juicy fruit, which is useful as a table grape and in juice, jelly, something called "hull pie" (crust, Muscadines, and meringue; I kid you not), and wine. It thrives in heat and needs fewer days of cold than other wine grapes, a quality not to be sneered at when we come to the topic of wine and climate change. The relatively mild winters of Arkansas provide just the right amount of stress to produce great wine out of Muscadines.

The Post Winery dominates the wine landscape in Altus and Ozark, the town next door. One way the winery accomplishes this dominance is with beautifully carved and designed road signs erected up and down the byways of the wine region. During the weekend grape festival, the Post was packed, with customers lined up at the three cash registers; boxes of wine being taped and sent out the door; customers seated at the adjoining Trellis café, waiting for paninis; and visitors, myself included, lined up at the tasting counter.

The sparkling Muscadine wine called Blue Parachute is one of the Post's best-selling wines. So I had to taste that, and it was worthy of its fame. I never got to taste Catawba sparkling wine, the queen of the Ohio Valley, but I imagine it had many of the same qualities—fruity sweetness, zest, a little layering. Here we are, over a hundred years after the time of Nicholas Longworth, rediscovering the possibility of a native grape to give us a decent, maybe even great, Champagne.

As much as I like the Blue Parachute, I was even more impressed with the still white Muscadine wine. In fact, the Altus/Ozark wine region seems to have zoomed in on Muscadine, at least in recent years. Tina Post confirms this in a phone interview. To my great surprise, the Post Winery, where she wears many hats, has mostly deprioritized growing and bottling Cynthiana.[5]

Though she does not speak for every winery in Arkansas's wine regions, Post more or less handed the baton of Norton/Cynthiana over to Missouri. The grape simply grows better there, she thinks. Her brother Thomas Post, vineyard manager for many years and now vineyard consultant, used to sell up to forty thousand Cynthiana plants a year, mostly to Missouri.[6]

Post allows that Norton/Cynthiana has a following, but the market for a Post Cynthiana simply isn't there. "I'm a dry red drinker. It's something I could drink. We made a good one. But we couldn't sell it," she says. "If they don't take off, you have to get something that's marketable."[7]

Unlike Cabernet, which everyone loves, Post says, Cynthiana is polarizing. People either love it or actively dislike it. "I poured some yesterday for a gentleman, and he said, 'That's really different.' But he didn't buy it," she relates. That said, Post says that the Post vineyard will probably always grow some Cynthiana, as a matter of tradition. There might be a Cynthiana blend of some kind in the winery's future, she intimates.[8]

By contrast, the Post's Muscadine wine has performed very well. According to Post, Muscadines grow best in the foothills of Arkansas, which is the northernmost range in which the grapes will grow. That tracks with what I have been learning about the need for grapes to "struggle" for their survival. "They just grow really well here," Post says. "It's like cooking. You have to have good ingredients." The secret to making a great Muscadine wine didn't arrive gift wrapped, though, Post says. "We've learned just a lot with the process. We were on a big learning curve, beginning in the 1960s."[9]

To make the kind of wine they make with native grapes, the Post has invested heavily in its equipment. Post throws around terms like *cold-fermentation tanks* and *crossflow filtration*. They remove excess oxygen during bottling with a nitrogen drip. And the wine is stored at a perfectly stable, cool temperature before being transported.[10]

To my surprise, Post says she did not always plan to make her career at the family winery. She started out in the fitness industry. But then she had an idea for a little restaurant and café, which is now the wildly successful Trellis Room. She is very knowledgeable about the nutritional benefits of wine. "The Muscadine is one of the most nutraceutical beneficial fruits in the world. I tell people to eat the skins and seeds because they are a powerhouse of ellagic acid and resveratrol—even more than is contained in the pulp," she says. "The juice has it too. It'll cure what ails you," she says. The Post produces very popular Concord wines—table and port. People like it because it is sweet, but not syrupy, she says. It also features 19 percent alcohol. "I call it an American-style port," Post says.[11]

Tina Post is a descendant of Jacob Post, who planted his Arkansas vineyard in 1880. It was the first vineyard in the state, and it was a mere seven or eight acres. The business has expanded greatly since then. Post is among the fifth generation of family members to take up a position there. Her nephew, James, works on the farm, and her niece, Terese, is the chef. Her brother Thomas is the vineyard consultant. Another brother, John, is the president and CFO; a sister Rosemary is the secretary, graphic artist, and photographer, producing the art for labels and package design, along with another sister, Jacqueline, who also manages chain accounts. Over the years, all of the family has worked in the business.

Over the years, the Posts obtained a little notoriety. Jacob, the patriarch who emigrated from Switzerland, got into trouble for selling to a minor, as was reported in the 1986 German paper *The Echo*. He was exonerated because there was an adult present for the sale. His daughter-in-law, Katherine, maintained a little still during Prohibition. "She served food. Then she would fill their jug for a dime," Post explains. Katherine was busted for selling to a couple of revenuers. "The revenuers are always there," says Post.[12]

Both family members received pardons, but Post has a drawing of her grandmother, a smallish woman, on the June 22, 1929, front page of the *St. Louis Post Dispatch* in handcuffs next to a U.S. marshal. She claimed that her short stint in jail was the best vacation she ever had because it came with a reprieve from running a business and raising several children.[13]

The Post family weathered Prohibition with a little moonshining, and they were allowed to make wine for use in church sacraments. During our phone chat, Post took a beat to mourn the loss of all the other smaller wineries in Altus that shut down and didn't reopen after Prohibition. "Who knows what would have happened to the area if prohibition hadn't come along," she notes.[14]

Post and I found a lot of common ground joking about the wine snobs. She had quite a few good one-liners. "They grow Moscato, but turn up their noses at Muscadine and Concord," she says. "Well, now wait a minute. I just kind of have to laugh. Are you kind of thinking about what you're saying? Live for the day. Seize the day and stop at different wineries, there's so much there with the history. It's just fun, like different ice creams."[15]

Drinking only *Vitis vinifera* is fine, but it's like eating only one food, she says. "Step away from your tightly held cultural beliefs, try regional wines and the unfamiliar varietals, it's really okay. There's a whole big world out there." I enjoyed the Chateau Aux Arc hybrid Savant on my own in my beautiful Airbnb room over a couple of nights, and that was the only Cynthiana I could find during the entire trip.[16]

6

The Screaming Canary

Some time in my forties, I lost my appetite for apples. They were so mealy! I tried different brands. I switched from Delicious to McIntosh to Honeycrisp to Granny Smith, trying to find the kind of apples I loved as a child. Perhaps it was the presentation. I got two different mandolines for quickly cutting them into slices. But the slices were also disappointing. I concluded that I just didn't know how to shop for apples.

Has my palate changed? I like wine a lot more than I did in my thirties. I developed a taste for blue cheese. I switched from milk chocolate to dark chocolate, the darker and unsweeter the better. I have been known to snack on straight up baker's chocolate. So maybe my taste was becoming just too damn sophisticated?

But I still adore nearly all the *other* things I loved in childhood: French toast, spaghetti with meatballs, slaw dogs, brownies. Why would apples be any different?

Finally, the *Christian Science Monitor* explained it to me. A forty-year Japanese study of apples found that climate change has altered their essential chemistry. As a result of overall warmer weather, apples are now sweeter—but softer. Their quotas of malic acid have also declined.[1] What this means for your average "apple a day; keep my doctor at bay" folks is that it's much harder to find an apple that delivers that tart crunch. If the two things you value most in an apple are its tartness and snap, you may, like me, have given up finding the apple of your dreams. So it should come as no surprise that climate change is also slowly altering grapes and, by association, wine.

In France's illustrious Bordeaux region, grapes now ripen faster due to the longer, hotter summers, and these riper grapes contain more natural sugar.

This produces a bolder flavor that was, in its day, highly valued. But what is really interesting about the increase in sugar is that it makes the wine more alcoholic. This, to some, might sound like a good thing, but the reviews are mixed.

This would probably be a good time to remind you that I am neither a wine expert nor, by any stretch, a connoisseur. I have never met a bottle of wine that I couldn't drink. I have met and even unintentionally purchased bad wine, mind you, but never a wine that could not be salvaged with several slugs of bourbon, some cold green tea, and sliced fruit. It turns out Rachel Ray published a recipe for Kentucky sangria much like mine in 2016, so I can't prove I thought of it first.

So. When I learned that French Bordeaux is becoming more potently intoxicating, I'm afraid my first, entirely unsophisticated response was "Bring it." But this is not how the wine connoisseurs and real wine writers feel. Apparently, these more-finely-tuned-than-me experts have drawn a firm line in the sand between 14 percent and 15 percent alcohol content in French wine. L. J. Johnson-Bell, who writes of the intersection between wine and climate, objects to a 15 percent alcohol Bordeaux: "If it's over 14 percent alcohol, it's not wine, I say."[2]

To the real wine writers, over 14 percent alcohol blots out the more important features of wine. The words *balance, layering, texture, subtlety,* and *flavors* usually get used here. Some wine drinkers think wine that is too heavy with alcohol may as well be vodka. Above the 14 percent mark, wine loses its distinction as wine, they think.

It's pretty well known, especially among the makers of prison gin, that adding plain white sugar to a batch of booze is a quick and dirty way to make the alcohol content stronger. Twice the buzz. And no need to study. So I was surprised to learn that, way back when, around the time I was a child, the estimable winemakers in Bordeaux were allowed to put sugar in their wine, and it was not considered cheating. This not only boosted the buzz; it also heightened the structure and complexity of the wine. The French government, which has *a lot* to say about how French wine is made, permitted this with no apparent demure.

Over the years, as planet earth warmed up, the Bordeaux grapes became naturally sweeter, and the vintners did not need to add sugar. There was a golden age of French wine, maybe in the '90s, when the grapes were perfect, juicy and naturally sweet, but not encroaching on territory that is rightfully occupied by tequila. Now, with the planet warmed up to the point of clear and present danger, that sweetness is damaging the essential nature of French wines, the experts feel.

I have to confess that stressing out about whether French wines are crossing over into 15 percent alcohol content feels a little like playing violin on the lip of an active volcano. I mean, it's kind of fascinating that the French and their wine lovers care desperately about that fatal 1 percent of alcohol, but there are parts of the world that are literally on fire while whole civilizations are being flooded out of existence.

Wine grapes are interesting, though, because they have been changing in response to a hotter planet for many decades now. The vineyards of the world have been screaming at us about the weather, but their screams were silent, and the people who could hear those screams had little power to implement change.

Vineyards Feel Changing Weather First

In the lingering denial years, around 1995–2015, while Fox News and *South Park* were convincing Americans and anyone else who would listen that climate change was a hoax, vineyard owners around the Old World were already quietly wondering, not if climate change were real, but how they were going to deal with it. They are and have quietly been for some time on the frontier of climate change adaptation.

About the remnants of climate change denial, L. J. Johnson-Bell writes, "Their ignorance is an insult to the millions of highly competent wine industry professionals who are up to their elbows in hard evidence."[3] For the Europeans, the proof of climate change was in their grapes, if nowhere else. In fact, wine grapes are almost as good as ice core samples for giving an unimpassioned view of climate history. While scientists stationed in Antarctica and Greenland were patiently coring icebergs, almost certainly to the derision of their friends and family, they were metaphysically working alongside an ally: grape growers.

The wine grape is a difficult crop to grow. There is a narrow band of summer temperatures that allow it to thrive. As well, it must have a cold enough winter so that the vines go dormant annually. But wine grapes are among the most profitable of crops. So grape farmers and winemakers keep detailed records about what worked and what didn't. And temperatures, soil quality, rainfalls, droughts, and extreme weather events are all carefully recorded, year after year. For the European wine industry, this means we have reliable records going back decades. These records bring us round to the same conclusion as the ice core scientists. The earth is changing. While there have always been weather swings and extreme events, the overall temperature of the planet has been rising, and the events are getting more extreme and more frequent.

Perhaps no wine family in the world has kept better records than the Valentini family, which has grown grapes and made wine in the Abruzzo region of Italy since 1650. Johnson-Bell describes the Valentini family as "the most elusive, enigmatic, and quality-obsessed to exist in wine-making history."[4] They use only a small portion of their own grapes, selling the majority. With their carefully selected grapes, they make exactly three different wines: a legendary Trebbiano d'Abruzzo and two Montepulcianos. Their processes are a matter of speculation, with one wine retailer positing that the grapes are crushed in cement vats and aged in old, possibly ancient Slovenian oak casks.[5]

The Valentini wine is a near-perfect coal mine canary because the family uses none but traditional methods. They do nothing to alter acidification or the temperature at which the wine ferments. They do no filtration, and their wines are free of added must and lactic bacteria. Because of this commitment to very old artisanal practices, their grapes and wines are especially vulnerable to permanent shifts in weather.

Of particular note are the family's extant written records dating back to 1817. These records spell out the story of a gradually but inexorably warming Abruzzo region. Of special interest are the Valentini vineyard harvest dates. In the online publication *Ciencia & Vinho*, Paula Silva writes, "The maturation of the grapes always fell around the middle of October for over 140 years . . . in the last forty years, instead, there was a constant increase of the advance with grapes ready to be harvested as early as the end of August."[6]

A 2019 study conducted by Pennsylvania State University in collaboration with Italian scientists also showed a shift in rain patterns. Though the Abruzzo region gets roughly the same average rainfall yearly, that rain falls on fewer and fewer days as time wears on. That means that, instead of moderate and light rains, the region's rain often comes down hard, and hard rains can damage crops.[7]

Wine, climate scientists agree, is the canary in the coal mine. When the climate is bad enough to kill wine grapes, we are in trouble. It would be lovely if this were a problem confined to society's elite who drink a bottle of wine per two people and complain that no one wants to work anymore. Lamentably, that is not the case. We need the same soil, water, and reliable temperatures to grow our food. Where wine is admittedly nothing but a luxury, other crops are not. If we listen closely enough and with our metaphoric ears, wine is singing to us that the path we are on may seem safe enough, but if we keep going this way, it is going to kill us.

The mainstream media are now mostly conceding the reality of climate change, though still waffling on how often a killing heat wave or cyclone is climate-change related. Statistics on the lethality of climate change vary widely, of course, depending on who you read. The World Health Organization reported fifteen thousand climate-related deaths in 2022, but it counted only those people who died from extreme heat. In 2021, Bloomberg reported that climate change was killing five million people a year. "Almost 10% of global deaths can be attributed to abnormally hot or cold temperatures," that vehicle declares.[8] Rebecca Hersher of National Public Radio notes that high and low temperatures are not the only ways climate change kills. Floods and raging fires are also the outcome of a warming planet, and they claim lives.[9] Where food is scarce, droughts can cause starvation. And science is still catching up to how climate change abets the spread of disease.

The worst impacts are absorbed by the poorest people. When a hurricane or cyclone hits Zimbabwe, Puerto Rico, or the Bahamas, the poorest residents have little recourse against the destruction of their homes, crops, and water supply. Their sketchy infrastructure collapses easily, and their safety net has gaping holes. Their mechanisms for recovery are inadequate.

Perhaps it seems elitist to write about the impacts of climate change on the wine industry. I mean, who cares if French Merlot is in trouble when people are actually dying? When whole civilizations are literally going underwater. The Guna Yala people, for example, are but one island culture that now has to depart for the mainland or drown. They must leave their ancestral home of Crab Island, off the coast of Panama, because rising sea levels are destroying all they built. The Guna Yala did not contribute to climate change. They have no cars or major industry. They didn't deforest. Hundreds of years ago, their ancestors sailed to Crab Island to escape the Spanish invaders. Now, they are being displaced again as melting ice floes swell the ocean and slowly drown the place they've called home for centuries. And yet here I am, writing about wine. So, if you put this book down in disgust with its triviality, I respect that decision.

If you are still reading, you should know that the French wine industry had incontrovertible proof that climate was tampering with wine way back in 2006. In that year, a major winemaking district petitioned French president Nicolas Sarkozy to allow vineyards to be irrigated.

To understand why irrigation was, at that time, against Appellation d'Origine Contrôlée (AOC) regulations and even those of the European Union, we must understand that successful wine is the result of struggle. Wine grapes need summer warmth and winter cold. They must experience something *like* death—the annual winter dormancy of the vines is akin to a coma—in order to bring a great fall harvest. Furthermore, to achieve the longevity that French grapevines have achieved, the vines must send their roots far down into the earth, more or less straight down, not sideways or at an angle. Vines that have deep, deep roots are curmudgeonly and hard to kill. They can survive a drought because they search out and drink up water that is hiding several feet below the planet's crust. This survival mechanism explains why food crops will wither and die in a moderate drought, but the grapevines will mutter and give their owners the silent treatment, then spring back to life after a good rain.

However. If the vines can find water more easily, say through an irrigation ditch, then the roots will not work so hard to find the moisture. Those roots may grow sideways, parallel to the topsoil, instead of plunging downward. Similarly, fertilization lures grape roots away from their instinct to delve. When all the resources are readily available on the surface, the roots will do some quiet quitting. They will be shallow. This makes the whole plant vulnerable. Vines with shallow roots are not set up to survive droughts, hard frosts, hard rains, hail, or other injuring events. Deep roots are the grape's insurance against injury. Shallow-rooted vines die early and often. Then the vines have to be replanted. This costs the vineyard heavily, because it takes at least three years for new vines to produce a profitable wine. There is a reason that old vines are respected by winemakers and connoisseurs alike.

This problem is well known to French vintners. And that's why it was a major turning point for grape farmers to ask for irrigation. But, without that handout, wine in the Languedoc-Roussillon region might have disappeared. Sarkozy caved, and irrigation was allowed. And it continues to be allowed today, though there are regulations.

Hailstorms

Shallow roots are probably not going to kill French wine by themselves. That privilege belongs to hailstorms. Do a casual internet search for "hail destroys French wine grapes" and you will see a plethora of news articles—spanning many years. Chateau Lassegue, owned by Pierre and Monique Seillan, Jess Jackson, and Barbara Banke, was devastated by hail in 2009. At first, it seemed their crop was ruined. Their consultants told them to scrap the crop, cut back the vines, and hope for a better year next time.

However, Pierre Seillan believed that, if he cut his vines, they would be vulnerable to yet another danger—untimely frost. The exposed vines could die. He put his faith in the deep roots of his old, unirrigated vines. He and his son instructed their staff to carefully prune away all the damaged leaves and buds. Their vines yielded a smaller crop, but they *had* a crop that year. And as is often true of grapes that have had to fight for their survival, the resulting wine was delicious and highly praised.

That 2009 hailstorm was in no way unique. In 2013, a nine-minute hailstorm devastated the Bordeaux wine region's vineyards again. The hail tore through the old wood, breaking vines and decimating leaves and fruit. Some vineyards resembled skeletons; the vines were so bare. Approximately a third of the region's harvest was lost.

Most vineyards in France are owned by families and small entrepreneurs, not corporations. The cost of insuring their crops against hail was too high for many of these growers, and a large part of them could not make insurance claims, as a result. The *Guardian* estimated the cost to be about a hundred million euros. That esteemed publication also estimated the loss of one job per five ruined hectares of wine grapes.[10]

Hail struck Bordeaux and nearby Charentais again in 2018, and some described it as the worst of its kind for thirty years. Either there is a lack of historical perspective among newsagents reporting on French wine country or the hail is getting exponentially worse. French vineyards are also at the mercy of late frosts, heat waves, and hard rains, which can swell the fruit, leaving it less flavorful.

Another consequence of climate change is that varietals now tend to ripen at the same time. Traditionally, French grape farmers grew Pinot Noir, Merlot, and Cab Sav, and they all came to fruition at different times of the growing season. This provided some security against damaging weather. Even if the Merlot crop were lost due to hail, for instance, the Cab Sav might survive because it had not yet fruited.

To offset the danger of all grapes ripening simultaneously, new wine varietals have been introduced and made eligible for AOC certification. These include Arinarnoa, Castets, Marselan, and Touriga Nacional. Presumably, these new varietals introduce more insurance against the loss of the more historic vines. Different subspecies will weather disease, hail, severe rains, and frosts differently. For vineyard owners, it's a case of hedging one's bets.

Ancient *Vitis vinifera* vines have weathered wars, religious strife, and bad leadership, but climate change now threatens an industry that is thousands of years old. And France is not alone. All over Europe, wine production is down 20 percent since 2013. Drought, water shortages, excessive heat, and unpredictable frosts are killing the continent's grapes.

Peter Is Robbed, but Paul Is Paid

Are there any upsides to a warmer climate? Of course there are! Canada now has a well-established wine industry, and even Denmark is getting in on the game. The south of England has become an actual contender (as opposed to a tired joke) in the international wine scene. Imagine James Herriot of *All Creatures Great and Small* driving through the Dales, which are now crowded with rows of vineyards, and you will have the approximate picture. Nature has stolen from Peter and paid Paul. France's losses are English gains.

According to Lyme Bay Winery, winemaking in Great Britain dates back to 43 AD, when those corrupting influencers, the Romans, introduced the art of viticulture to the innocent Anglo-Saxons. Winemaking was retired, however, during the Great Wars because land was needed to raise food.

In the twenty-first century, however, British winemaking has come back full throttle. To pretend that a changing climate had nothing to do with this would be very naive. In 2019, NBC bravely reported that climate change had turned the south of England into the perfect territory for making sparkling wine.[11] Readers of my generation may remember the jokes about how wet London used to be. The quintessential Englishman wore a bowler hat *and* carried an umbrella over it to keep both head and hat dry. An entire line of prestige clothing—London Fog—was named after the moisture in southern England.

Well, England is nowhere near that wet now. The wine grape harvest of 2018 was so abundant that vineyard employees were reduced to storing excess wine in a parking lot. English vineyards yielded 15 percent more wine than was expected. And the quality was high, at least according to the people who produced it: "The quality across the board is fantastic," enthuses Christopher White, CEO of Denbies.[12]

In 2022, the University of East Anglia published a report that predicted English winemaking would continue to expand and flourish for at least the next twenty years. According to that report, there were, on publication, eight hundred vineyards in the United Kingdom. The 2018 bumper crop produced 15.6 million bottles. East Anglia attributed these facts to the 1 percent rise in temperature across much of the kingdom. There was an as-yet not-fully-tapped potential for growing still wine grapes, the report went on to say, mentioning Pinot Noir and Chardonnay.[13]

Savvy English winemakers know that their results are based on climate changes, and they also know that what changed could change again—disastrously. Their interviews emphasize the need for vigilance. "They'll have to keep very close to what is going on with the weather and adapt things. One year they'll be flooded and one year they'll be irrigating," says Chris Foss, who heads the wine department at Plumpton College.[14] The smart English winemakers will also be aware that frosts in early spring will put early budding grapevines at risk for loss.

One newish maker of English sparkling wine notes that making wine in Britain is not easy street. "Certainly, we've had more vicious, harder rainstorms and gales. I mean, I grew up in England, and I don't remember ever having such gales and rainstorms as we have now," says Bella Spurrier, founder of Bride Valley, a Dorset-based maker of sparkling wine, in an interview with Brian Freedman.[15]

The English winemakers also seem smartly poised to change grape species as needed. "I don't think we can pin down a particular English wine just yet, and why would we?" asks Sam Lindo, who makes wine at Camel Valley. Though thoroughly optimistic in his interview with Wine Enthusiast, Lindo also has some sense of an end date for all this: "We are where champagne was in the 1950s," he notes, adding, "We have a long way to go until we will experience the difficulties they are experiencing now."[16]

One thing the English winemakers have going for them is their keen awareness that their good fortune is largely the result of a planetary change that could be disastrous in the end. They also have the good fortune to have overcome the snobbery that surrounds wine not made in continental Europe or California. Unlike American midwesterners, who will go to a package store and buy a bottle from New Zealand when their local winery is two miles away, the English have happily embraced their own sparklers and have lovingly nicknamed it "English fizz."

Is it their proud national identity that allows the English to love the wine they're with? One can only guess. "I think that the quality has been going up, and people have stopped thinking of English wine as a joke because it really is okay," says Spurrier modestly.[17]

Adam Williams, who directs sales at the Kentish Balfour Winery, thinks this trend exists across the European wine countries. In Spain, wine drinkers are loving on Cava, the Spanish sparkling wine. In Italy, they are drinking more Franciacorta, which is an Italian Champagne. Williams says: "So this drinking-local thing is a global trend within sparkling wine."[18] The English are busy making lemonade out of French lemons. They have accomplished amazing things in only thirty years, the resurgence of English wine dating back to the 1990s.

In the United States, Vermont is similarly fortunate. Vermont's yearly temperature average has increased by two and a half degrees since 1970, and its rainfall has increased by 21 percent since 1900. Meanwhile, Vermont's legacy dairy industry is suffering from falling prices and rising overhead. It may come as little surprise that some Vermont growers pivoted to growing grapes and making wine. Snow Farm Vineyard & Winery was the first brave business to try its fortunes in the deep north in 1997. Today, there are at least twenty wineries in the Great Cheese State. Vermont growers are capitalizing on the development of new hybrid wines that can survive a New England winter: Vignoles, Traminette, Frontenac, Vidal Blanc, and Baco Noir as well as the traditional European Chardonnay and Riesling.

However, the canary is screaming pretty loudly that, if growers in Vermont and England are having bumper crops of wine grapes, we are in for some trouble down the road. There's no doubt that the wine industry could abandon all the historic wine regions and go north. If the planet keeps warming, grapes could potentially grow in melting permafrost. But they mustn't. There is only so much land. If the earth keeps heating up, and we have to choose between growing food and growing wine, I do hope we will choose food. Also, farming destroys wildlife habitats and leads to plummeting populations, even the extinction of animals.

Every international climate change agreement must limit the expansion of wine grapes into previously untapped territories. I say this as a wine lover. We can't afford to keep drinking wine at the expense of everything else.

Will Napa Survive?

I confess to having started this book with a prejudice against California and, to a lesser extent, France and Italy. "Too long have they rested on their laurels!" I thought. My Prairie Home Companion mentality told me that midwesterners and rural Americans work harder, and yet our wine has been snubbed. (I consider northern Kentucky part of the Midwest. Face it. I can walk to Indiana from my house.) My Three Sisters Cynthiana is just as good as, if not better than, any wine I've had from California. I pitched this book to my publisher with words like "California gets all the attention. And they don't deserve it." That was before I knew how bad things were in California. Now my heart is breaking.

Like France's vineyards, California's wine industry faces the threats of unpredictable weather and water shortages along with runaway wildfires and damaging smoke from fires. In 2021, the *New York Times* reported on a vineyard owner whose extensive fire damage caused his insurance company to cancel his policy. No other company would insure him either. His quandary is not unusual among California's wine growers. When they are insurable, they may or may not be able to afford the policy. After the 2020 Glass Fire, named after the nearby Glass Mountain, one vineyard owner reported that his insurance premium went up to $1 million a year, five times what he had paid the year before.[19]

The same article reported that, off the main roads, Napa Valley looked like a burned-out disaster area with water shortages and nervous wreck winemakers. Winery owner Christoper Chappellet was quoted as saying that, if the drought and heat continue to worsen, "all of us are out of business."[20]

Napa Valley winemakers may have the dubious distinction of having invented the term *smoke taint*. This is the damage that smoke, even from a faraway fire, can do to a row of grapes. Laboratory analysis confirms that smoke can penetrate the grape skin and damage the taste of the wine. Red grapes are much more at risk for smoke taint because their skins become part of the wine, as opposed to white grapes, whose skins are removed in the winemaking process. Red grapes are also harvested later, putting them literally in the line of fire, wildfires being more likely to rage in the fall when red grapes get harvested. This is a problem for grape growers who are used to selling red grapes for approximately twice what white grapes sell for.

The winemakers of Southern California have a saying: Cabernet is king. Whether Cabernet can afford to be king for much longer remains to be seen. California grape growers have resorted to mitigations that might sound like madness. Some growers are spraying their crops with sunscreen, hoping to prevent scorching. Another tactic is to buy treated wastewater, recycled from flushed toilets and sinks, and use it to water crops. In an era where rainwater is nonexistent and reservoirs are mud pits, it makes sense.

Getting answers from the internet can be an exercise in futility, as I'm sure you know, dear readers. With trepidation, I googled "Will California wine survive climate change?" As you might expect, there was no consensus. Less than a year previous to this moment in which I am banging away on my Chromebook, Bloomberg published an article titled "California's $45 Billion Wine Industry Faces Climate Peril."[21]

To that, *Forbes* clapped back with the headline "Why California's $46 Billion Wine Industry Is Better Prepared for Climate Change Than Some of Its Competitors?" A closer look at the *Forbes* article shows that survival for California wine is, according to reporter Steven Savage, all about adaptation. California is better poised to survive because "it has more potential to adapt because it is not as tradition bound as the famous wine regions of Europe."[22]

Steven Savage duly notes the droughts, scorching, water shortages, wildfires, and smoke that are already threatening California. Then he mentions insects. During warmer weather, insects actually accelerate their life cycles, he writes casually, as my skin crawls. Then, as an afterthought, he explains that powdery mildew gets a leg up with warmer weather.

But all that was in 2022. What about this year? Right now? While I am tapping, tapping, t-a-p-p-i-n-g away on my Chromebook? In January of this year, Tim Carl wrote that the roller coaster metaphor for California wine is no longer apt. It's more like "a rocket ship navigating through an asteroid storm in some high budget action film."[23]

Dr. Megan Bartlett, a plant biologist and assistant professor at the University of California, Davis, was a lot calmer. She assured me that California's wine industry would survive. Growers and winemakers understand that there are challenges, and they are working to address them. "Even if climate change stopped tomorrow, we'd still be an industry that deals with many challenges," she points out. "There are also a lot of pieces that are independent of climate change."[24]

California's wildfires aren't started by climate change, Bartlett notes. In fact, she believes that human interactions with the natural world, like "arcing power lines and garbage burns that get out of control," are responsible for the increase in fires, for the most part. An expanding electrical infrastructure poses a fire risk. However, once a fire ignites, the dryness and wind caused by climate change can make the fire spread faster and blaze harder. Climate change doesn't cause fire, but it causes what Bartlett calls "fire weather." "That puts us back in the driver's seat more—even if we're dealing with an environmental context that makes fires worse, we can control the human actions that start fires," she notes. Bartlett herself has done extensive research on how plants weather a drought. She even developed a screening mechanism to help researchers and grape breeders quickly know how drought tolerant a grape species will be.[25]

Over time, California grape growers will have to diversify and consider a broader range of wine grape species. She concedes, though, that weaning Napa Valley away from Cabernet will not be easy. "I think it's going to be difficult to break that association between variety and place. Our industry is based on associations like that in a way that Europe isn't. Right now, it doesn't make sense to plant much besides Cab in Napa," Bartlett says.[26]

Fortunately, rootstocks can be varied and updated, allowing Cabernet to be grafted onto hardier roots that can better withstand heat, drought, bugs, and disease. It should come as no surprise that grape scientists have been developing rootstocks closely based on native American vines, especially *Vitis rupestris*, *Vitis riparia*, *Vitis berlandieri*, and *Vitis × champinii*. "I think the cutting edge of rootstock breeding is branching out from these species," Bartlett says. "Those four have been the foundation of the rootstocks we have to date, but there's a lot more diversity that we haven't used yet, including species that live in very dry areas or are already resistant to important diseases." Examples include *Muscadinia rotundifolia*, the Muscadine vine and *Vitis rufotomentosa*, which I was very interested to learn about because it is a variant of *aestivalis*. "Historically, we aimed for lots of light on the fruit," she says. But that has to change because of the overall hotter growing seasons. A lot can be done with how vines are trellised, Bartlett notes. Some growers are looking into shade cloths. Spacing vines farther apart and improving soil conditions are also good tools in the war against drought and rising temperatures. "The more organic material you have in the soil, the better it holds water," she says.[27]

Growers can also use drones and other sophisticated technology to pinpoint where in their vineyard the vines are most stressed. Vines on an incline or on thinner soil, for instance, might be the first to die during a drought. Knowing exactly where to hydrate a vineyard will help growers keep their vines healthy while also conserving water.

The Damage in South Africa

It might be tempting to scoff a little at the millionaire vineyard owners of California. "Poor little rich kids," I hear you sneering, dear reader. Or, wait, no, that's the Marxist voice in my own head talking. But the damage climate change does to wine is not just a problem for the elite. In South Africa, the wine industry has offered pathways to prosperity for Black South Africans in the wake of apartheid. But now that inclusive industry is in danger.

South Africa is one of the most fascinating wine cultures in existence today. Fascinating because, let's face it, most wine culture is pale, pale white. When wine writer Brian Freedman visited South Africa in 2014, he was surprised to see so many Black citizens employed in nearly all levels of winemaking and distribution. Many were sommeliers, others managed stores and tastings, and many were winemakers. What they were not were landowners.[28]

That is changing, though, albeit with aching slowness. Paul Siguqa of South Africa acquired a vineyard in 2019 and became the owner of the first South African winery to be entirely Black owned and Black run. His is a true rags-to-riches story. His mother was in the wine industry, as a farmhand. Growing up, Siguqa hated the vineyard that left her exhausted at the end of the day. Often, she was paid in wine, a tradition that was outlawed in the '60s but somehow persisted into the '90s.

Within this deeply flawed system, however, there was some mobility. Siguqa went to college, paid for in part by a job he got serving wine. That job gave him another perspective on the wine industry. He saw Black South Africans relaxing and socializing with glasses of wine. Wine quit being his nemesis and became his dream. He saved up for fifteen years, then bought the land he needed to grow grapes and make his own wines.

A 2023 article in the *New York Times* reports that only 3 percent of South Africa's wine grape acreage is Black owned, but there are at least eighty-two Black-owned brands of wine.[29] That is a 20 percent increase since 2019. Freedman wrote, in 2022, that 60 percent of South Africans employed in the wine industry were from "previously disadvantaged Black and mixed-race groups."[30] Unfortunately, this thriving and inclusive industry is at risk from rising temperatures. South Africa is heating up—well, everywhere is heating up—but South Africa is heating up faster, for some reason.

According to the U.S. Agency for International Development, temperatures in South Africa have risen twice as fast as the global average, and this has been going on since the 1990s. A major contributing factor is the country's dependence on coal.[31] South Africa's agriculture, in particular, is vulnerable to water shortages, rainfall variability, a climate-related increase in pests and disease, and unpredictable weather that wreaks havoc on growing and harvesting schedules. However, while many crackpots in the United States still enjoy rolling their eyes any time "climate change" is mentioned, it became real for South Africans in 2018. Shortages of rainfall over three years left even the wealthiest residents of Cape Town skipping showers, skipping flushes, and recycling shower water in toilets.

An individual's right to water is enshrined in the South African Constitution, which guarantees citizens twenty-five liters of water per day. With that fundamental right to water in mind, the South African government imposed water rationing of fifty liters per day, per person. For South Africa's winemakers, it was bad news indeed. The 2018 grape wine harvest was the smallest in a decade. The vines received approximately half the water they actually needed. In some grape-growing parts, the amount of water available for irrigation, supplied by dams, was down by 80 percent.

Add to that, discussions about whether vineyards were an essential industry, entitled to any water at all, had winemakers walking on eggshells. However, taking water away from agriculture is a dangerous thing to do, because it robs farmworkers of their jobs, exacerbating poverty and employment among, again, the most vulnerable people.

Wine as a Contributor to Climate Change

"Solutions" like toilet water for irrigation and sunscreen for grapes, if you can call them solutions, are way behind the curve. Vineyards and wineries are part of the climate change problem, and getting ahead of the curve is imperative. This means that vineyards and wineries must not only plan ahead to save wine from climate change; they must also save the planet from wine.

Robert Frost was a poetic genius, but was he also a prophet? He wrote the lines "Some say the world will end in fire / Some say ice."[32] He used "fire" as a metaphor for destructive passion, and "ice" for the kind of indifference that allows people to perish, the kind of indifference we see on the part of world leaders for poor communities that are already absorbing the brunt of climate change. In fact, the end of the world as we know it will likely be due to both fire *and* ice. Global warming is only one consequence of climate change. Severe storms, coastal and island flooding, drought and parching, and unpredictable swings of weather are other consequences.

The apparent contradictions of climate change—floods *and* drought, hotter summers *and* out-of-season cold snaps—are partly why some people still can't wrap their heads around its reality. When my friend Edwin runs his Labrador retrievers through the marshes of coastal Georgia on an unseasonably warm January day and then says "What's wrong with global warming?" I sigh with frustration. If only climate change were as benevolent as a warm day in winter.

Am I being histrionic? Will climate change really kill us? Well, probably not in my lifetime, but I am well into my sixties. The thing about climate change is that we can see the current consequences, but we have no idea what kind of timeline it's on. Mother Nature, brooding and angry with us, is withholding communication on this point.

To make things more interesting, climate change consequences are accelerating in some regions much faster than in others. Some business sectors, like wine, are feeling the pinch, while others, like technology, luxuriate in delayed reactions. We know that we are committed to a certain degree of sea level rise. But adjustments can be made, communities evacuated, seawalls constructed.

One of the key debates, among climate change scientists, is whether the permafrost will melt. Permafrost is more critical to our survival than icebergs even. When I attended a Climate Reality Project in 2017, one scientist declared that the permafrost would not melt. But recent reports from major news outlets all agree that the permafrost is melting, creating feedback loops that accelerate warming. I can't pretend to understand something better than the scientists who have been rigorously studying it for forty years or more. What I do understand is species extinction—which is a much easier concept for my humanities-trained brain to assimilate. Plant and animal species are declining at alarming rates all over the world. Climate change is a large part of that problem, though it is not the only cause.

The end of civilization is something I can be rather abstract about. It won't happen in my lifetime, and I've been really careful not to have descendants who would have utterly destroyed my current equanimity; I would have to worry about how the planet and my fellow humans would treat them after I am gone. But, for the disappearance of manatees and penguins, cave bats and frogs, orchids and bees, I wear a black armband around my heart every day.

Unfortunately, winemaking is a substantial contributor to climate change. Like other industries, it is putting too much carbon dioxide into the atmosphere. According to the Environmental and Energy Study Institute, agriculture, generally, accounts for 10 percent of climate change.[33] The International Panel on Climate Change sets that percentage much higher—at 23 percent.[34]

The transportation involved in winemaking and distribution is only one of the problems, but it is the biggest problem. Our snobbish preference for French wines or Spanish wines or Chilean wines or New Zealand wines means that these products become cargo. And that cargo gets flown or shipped across continents and oceans so that wealthy penthouse dwellers can pour it into glasses and brag about how it comes from too far away. The amount of spent jet fuel and other smog generated by importing wine from far away is a major contributor to the cumulative carbon dioxide that is killing us.

Wine also causes climate change by putting fungicides, pesticides, herbicides, and inorganic fertilizers into the soil and air. Runoff from the farms, carrying this mess of chemicals, then destroys the waterways. The glassmaking industry that supports wine distribution also claims its share of natural resources, creating air and water pollution. Making cork stoppers has caused the deforestation of cork trees. Even the paper labels on wine bottles come with a cost to the environment.

Before agriculture became a corporate affair, winemaking—in fact, all farming—was a much gentler industry. Daniel Norton didn't know what Roundup was, nor did Jean Jacques Dufour, so they were spared using it, as were all the farmers of the nineteenth century. For many decades, traditional winemakers swore off the use of chemicals and even irrigation on the grounds that it wasn't, well, traditional. In fact, the concept of terroir more or less demands organic practices. Terroir, not to be confused with terrorism, is the aspect of a wine that is unique because it comes from a unique soil with a unique water supply and a unique microclimate, including sun exposure, rainfall, and temperature.

Wine experts prattle a lot about terroir, and I can't believe I got this far into writing a book about wine without mentioning it. These experts say they can taste the soil and water that produced a specific wine. And they are not lying. The ability to pinpoint the exact region where a wine was made, by taste, is one of the qualifications of a master sommelier, possibly the hardest test to pass, and that's why the world's supply of master sommeliers is limited.

Corporate vineyards do the most damage, but they are also in a position to make constructive changes. Imagine the confusion of a small French winemaker when a megalithic wine corporation out of California—one that has been poisoning land and sea with truckloads of chemicals for decades—suddenly decides to cash in on the organic produce movement. Now, that corporation flagrantly markets itself as "sustainable," "organic," "green," and "earth friendly."

In addition to its old customers, it can now score thousands, possibly tens of thousands, of new customers who are drawn to its new environmentally friendly agenda. Of course, we should applaud the change either way; better late than never definitely applies to this situation, which is why I am naming no names. But I can't help imagining that French winemaker, the one who calls himself a farmer, exclaiming, "But I've been doing that all along!" Sustainable winemaking isn't all a matter of science and technology. Vineyards can achieve a lot of progress toward sustainability by simply reverting to what the earlier winemakers did—live with nature instead of conquering it.

Daniel Norton didn't have a commercial tiller. Today, it is commonplace to see a farmer or farmworker sitting astride a giant vehicle that is violently raking the soil behind him and kicking up a cloud of debris. Aggressive tilling, in which several inches of topsoil are turned over, makes a surprising contribution to climate change by fluffing dust, nitrous oxide, methane, and carbon dioxide into the air.

Commercial, machine-driven tilling depletes soil carbon and increases the risk of soil erosion. Furthermore, the machinery that is used for aggressive tillage is almost always powered by fossil fuels. And the use of that fuel is yet another way that wine grape growing contributes to climate change. Aggressive tilling is possibly the most damaging thing that farmers do, though chemical spraying and unsustainable water use certainly do harm as well. Despite the obvious benefits of conservative tilling, only half of the farmland in the United States is conservatively tilled, and only one-fifth of that land is untilled.

The main reason that so many farmers are still tilling aggressively is that it brings short-term results. Freshly plowed-up soil is mostly weed-free and loose enough to easily plant. This often results in good one-year yields. In other words, the quick money is in hard tilling. However, over time, such tillage destroys soil. Heavily tilled soil loses nutrients through runoff and erosion. And, where undisturbed soil will retain moisture, loose, aerated soil will not. The moisture in tilled soil evaporates quickly in heat and sun because it is not dense enough to hold on to water. Therefore, yearly tilling can force a farmer to replace the natural nutrients, lost with tilling, with chemical fertilizer. When topsoil loses its hydration because of overtilling, the farmer must then resort to irrigation.

The U.S. Department of Agriculture estimates that no-till farms, those that are not dragnetting the soil with diesel-powered plows, are saving the planet from 5.8 million tons of climate-changing carbon dioxide, the equivalent of taking a million cars off the road.[35]

Furthermore, no-till farming results in much richer soil because the remains of the last harvest—husks, leaves, stems, and stalks—remain on the surface of the soil instead of getting plowed under. These remains provide free fertilizer when left on the surface to mix with sun, soil, and rainfall. Earthworms, which are destroyed and disturbed with heavy tillage, further improve untilled soil health by participating in the carbon cycle.

It should, by now, be fairly obvious that no-till farming is a great long-term investment for the farmer. She saves money on the diesel needed to pull a tiller, saves money on water for irrigation, and also saves hugely on labor costs because not tilling requires no poorly paid and unhappy manual laborers. The Environmental and Energy Study Institute estimates that no-till farms save as much as 50 percent on the cost of labor.[36]

Where yields and profits are concerned, tilling allows farmers to make a quick buck. But that quick buck comes at the expense of soil health, and depleted soil costs more in the long run. Gene Branstool, who practiced no-till farming in central Ohio for thirty-eight years, told *U.S. News and World Report* that his yields were consistently higher than they would have been if he tilled.[37] Blaine Baker, a Michigan farmer, has been opting not to till for over twenty-three years on his family farm. His practices sometimes allow him to plant earlier than other farmers, Baker told environmental reporter Lester Graham.[38]

Untilled farmland performs best when crops are rotated and cover crops are employed to combat weeds and prevent erosion. "Our erosion is pretty much nil," since combining cover crops with non-tillage, Baker reports.[39] Weeds are the ongoing nemesis of the no-till farmer who may resort to herbicides to control them. However, even if chemicals are more often deployed in no-till farming, there's little doubt that it is, overall, a more sustainable practice. Randall Reeder, a retired agricultural engineer, goes so far as to say that climate change could be reversed if all the earth's farmland were converted to no-till.[40]

Wineries That Are Leading the Way

One vineyard that has taken the challenge of climate change seriously is Tabor Winery in Israel. In 2012, the Society for the Protection of Nature in Israel (SPNI) visited the winery and talked to manager Michal Akerman. What they saw, when SPNI visited, was a typical vineyard, geometric rows of trellised grapes with all other vegetation banished, wildlife banished, and soil sterilized and overfertilized. They used the term *monocropping* to describe how vineyards displace ecosystems. SPNI was strategic in approaching Akerman. By virtue of her PhD and her experience working in vineyards all over the world, she is Israel's first viticulturist.[41]

At that time, Akerman was used to pulling up dead vines and replanting. Dead vines were business as usual because irrigation and fertilizers had never encouraged the vines to root themselves deeply. Akerman had toured European vineyards and seen old vines; she knew the fruit from those plants was smaller but exponentially more flavorful and complex. By contrast, she knew that Israel's grapes were flat tasting.[42] She understood the connection between old vines and flavor. The average grapevine in Israel lived fifteen years. In Europe, it was normal for vines to be fifty years old, and some even lived to be one hundred.

Over the next nine years, Akerman worked on integrating nature back into her farm. She researched native plants. The four hundred trees she planted brought black bears back to the region. Strategically placed rock piles encouraged the return of storks, lizards, otters, chameleons, mice, and gophers. To deal with rodent incursions to the vineyard, she put up owl nest boxes. Cameras reveal owls feasting on mice and other predators that can damage crops.

The same cameras now confirm the presence of boar, foxes, wolves, and jackals who are allowed to roam the vineyards for much of the year. Though the vineyards are fenced, the fences are strategically left open during the parts of the year when the vines are not fruiting. The insects returned when the vineyard dialed back on herbicides and fertilizers. Tabor deployed an insect vacuum that the company used to study the mix of insect life and ensure that it was balanced. Akerman planted a low-lying ground cover between the grapevines. This lowers temperatures and keeps the grapes from cooking because the ground cover absorbs sunlight where bare soil bounces it back up into the grapes.

Amazingly, Tabor now makes do with almost no irrigation. Akerman's grapevines have deep roots. In an interview with *Forbes*, she betrays her excitement about what this could mean for vine longevity in Israel: "If we start to work like this, we will be able to talk about vines that are 40, 50, 60 years old. We will not have to replant after 15 years as the vines will be stronger, more vital and just more comfortable in their environment."[43] If you are like me, by now you are asking, But what about the wine!? Is the wine any good? This is what Freedman has to say: "Today, the wines that are grown on Tabor's land are expressive, incisive, energetic, and often haunting."[44]

Perhaps Akerman's greatest accomplishment, however, has been getting other grape growers to follow her lead. She intuited that there would be resistance to change. So she approached the younger growers first. When they had stronger vines, she was able to use that proof to convince the older growers to join in. Success is attractive and contagious, so other crops in Israel, like apricots, olives, and almonds, are now being grown under similar biodiverse conditions.

Tabor and its many associated growers have been so successful in fighting climate change for the wine industry that a contingent of French wine professionals visited in late 2022 to see if they could glean any secrets that would help France with their national wine emergency. They visited the Negev Desert's Pinto Winery. David Pinto, the winery's CEO, increased his year-over-year production from thirty thousand to sixty thousand bottles in 2022. What is highly impressive is that he did this in Israel's desert. A place where stones and sand dominate the bleak landscape. If wine can be made there, the French must reason, it should be possible to keep wine growing in France.

In the climate action community, there is an ongoing debate as to whether it is better to invest in solar and other alternative energy technologies or to plant native understory plants; route out invasive plant species, like kudzu; plant canopy trees; and focus on soil replenishment. The planting approach has the advantages of being relatively affordable and restoring habitat for wildlife as well as shade and beauty for humans. The advantage of wind and solar power is that they generate a lot of power without adding to the earth's carbon burden.

This debate can get a little vicious with the alternative energy proponents pointing out that trees can actually contribute to global warming if they are planted in places where they don't belong. The soil replenishers point out that the electricity used to charge electric cars often comes from coal, that wind turbines kill birds, and that trees are sometimes cut down to make room for solar panels.

In 2019, Ecowatch published an article declaring that "planting billions of trees is the best climate change solution available."[45] The next year, BBC shot back that "planting trees doesn't always help with climate change."[46] The article notes that trees introduce a dark canopy where they are planted, and the dark color attracts and traps heat from the sun. Since I'm not mincing words here, I'm just going to say it: vineyards and wineries need to do both. If you're part of the problem, you need to be part of the solution. Biodiversity, soil regeneration, wildlife, *and* solar and wind power.

Parducci Wine Cellars in Ukiah, California, has made it look easy. Their grapes are organically grown, and their power is sourced from 100 percent green energy, both wind and solar. They use biodiesel in their tractors. The jewel in Parducci's sustainability crown, though, is its water conservation system. Business partners Paul Dolan, Tim Thornhill, and Tom Thornhill launched a water reclamation project in 2006 that took two years to build. All the winery's wastewater is funneled into a man-made wetland where the grasses oxygenate the water and filter out debris such as metals and grape sugars. Aeration is achieved with waterfalls rather than motorized equipment, saving energy. The treated water is then used to irrigate the vineyard *and* provide water for wildlife in the nearby Russian River watershed. Tim Thornhill told *Wine Business* that the winery had reclaimed four million gallons of water for irrigation in one year.[47]

The company has also employed ground cover to replenish soil and foster biodiversity. As a result, birds and other insect predators keep the bug population under control and eliminate the need for pesticides. Sheep and pigs eat weeds and produce natural fertilizer. In 2008, the winery challenged other winemakers to follow suit and published *Parducci's Green Winegrowing Handbook*.[48] The company earned a Green-e certification and a 2009 Governor's Environmental and Economic Leadership Award. In 2015, the company took home an Eco Innovator Award from the Board of Equalization.

In New Zealand, the Grove Mill Winery is doing something similar. According to the *New Zealand Herald*, Grove Mill is the first carbon-neutral winery in the world, having achieved that status in 2006. Three hundred solar panels have helped the company reach that goal.[49] By 2009, six other New Zealand wineries had followed suit, achieving carbon-neutral status throughout the country's CarboNZero program, which allows businesses to offset some of their carbon dioxide emissions by purchasing credits from a lower carbon output business or multiple businesses. Carbon neutrality means that an individual or organization has quit contributing to climate change. It has transitioned from being the problem to being the solution.

Like Parducci, Grove Mill has created a wetland that benefits both water reclamation and the larger ecosystem, especially wildlife. Planting native species is an important part of the wetland conservation program. On a single planting day around 2020, the company planted seven hundred different species of plants.[50]

A company called FutureEcology helps Grove Mill track the biodiversity of the wetland. The goal for a healthy wetland is always to have the greatest variety of native species possible in a healthy balance. Solar panels and wetland restoration are business as usual for achieving sustainability. Where Grove Mill really had to get creative was in the packaging. Paper for the winery's labels is made from sugar cane, which grows fast and abundantly and makes a low-environmental-impact paper.

The company also uses bottles made from recycled glass that are lighter than traditional wine bottles. Bottle weight might not seem important until we consider that the main way wine production contributes to climate change is in transportation. Lighter bottles mean less weight on the vehicles that transport the product. Lower weight means less fuel has to be used in transportation. This is a huge innovation. Even the bottle caps at Grove Mill are manufactured locally, and they feature images of the wildlife that inhabit the nearby wetland. In 2020, Grove Hill winemaker Esme Holdsworth told *Dish* that some thought and effort went into designing the bottles. "We wanted to make sure the bottle was as beautiful and thoughtful on the outside as the quality of wine on the inside," she says.[51]

The label on Grove Hill's wines features the southern bell frog, an inhabitant of the nearby wetland. Frogs, famously, are indicator species, meaning their presence speaks to the overall health of an ecosystem. A system in which the amphibians have disappeared is in trouble in one or more ways. Holdsworth points out that the southern bell is the company's mascot, and individual frogs sometimes show up in the winery, where staff take the trouble of gently returning them to the wetland.

Readers may or may not be surprised to learn that Spain is taking a strong lead in studying the effects of climate change on its nation's wine. In an effort to understand the details of climate impacts, the Spanish government collaborates with the winemaking family Familia Torres, which grows grapes in the Catalan Pyrenees, Spain's northernmost eastern corner.[52] "Our objective," says the winery's website, "is to reduce our CO_2 emissions per bottle—from the vineyard to the end consumer—by 60% in 2030 to become a net zero emissions winery before 2040."[53]

As early as 2008, the winery founded the Torres & Earth program to raise climate awareness within the wine sector and society as a whole. As of this writing, Familia Torres had committed to erecting four solar panel arrays, within the year, to power the winery and the family's restaurant El Celleret.

The company has already implemented organic growing processes and has promised to implement "regenerative viticulture," which involves, among other things, deploying sheep to cut grass rather than mowing it with machines. Regeneration, as the Familia understands it, also means protecting biodiversity, with conservative soil management and the creation of wildlife corridors that protect native plant and animal species.

Miguel Torres Jr., the fifth Torres patriarch to run the family business, explains to Wine Enthusiast that biodiversity "translates to more insects, more birds, more amphibians and it contributes to creating a more resilient ecosystem."[54] Familia Torres has vineyards not only in Spain but also in Chile and California, giving the company a global and historical perspective on climate change impacts on the wine industry. The family planted trees over five thousand hectares in Chile to reforest an area that had been deforested in the nineteenth century in order to create farmland. In Chile, it should be noted, the wine industry is fighting hard against rapidly changing weather. Reforestation is critical to slowing and reversing that trend.

Perhaps the most interesting thing that Familia Torres has done is to explore and recultivate heritage grapes—that is, those that are native or of long-standing naturalization to the area. Miguel Jr.'s father, also a Miguel, began the quest for heritage grape species over forty years ago. At first, he was simply interested in the history of Catalonia wines. Then, as the ravages of climate change revealed themselves in earnest, it became a matter of preserving Spanish wine for future generations.

In the 1980s, the Torres family placed newspaper advertisements, asking readers to call in with any knowledge of ancestral grapes. It emerged that many minor wine grapes were lost during the phylloxera crisis. You remember phylloxera as the insect that decimated Europe's wine industry until rootstocks from the United States were used to save *Vitis vinifera*. The quest to find these heritage grapes took the Torres family into forests and beside creeks where the grapes had survived on their own, with no cultivating hand to guide or rescue them. No better testimony of a grape's resiliency exists than its ability to survive in the wild. Since the 1980s, the Torres family has rediscovered fifty-two grape species that would otherwise have been lost to history.

Only a few of those grapes were worth cultivating, and Miguel Jr. explains that the process of discovery to bottling takes seventeen years. The vines have to be cultivated over generations and freed from viruses. This involves taking cells from new shoots that crop up in spring. These new shoots are virus-free for a short time.[55]

These undiseased cells are then placed in petri dishes with nutrients that promote growth, and then the vines are grown in test tubes. The vines' next stage of growth is in a nursery, and then they are transplanted to an experimental garden where they compete with other species to become a Torres wine. One grape that passed all the tests to become a commercially produced wine is the Forcada.

The Torres family also makes a point of sharing rediscovered varietals with other vineyards. According to the company website, in 2016, the company decided to bottle wine made from the Moneu grape.[56] Named after a Spanish river, Moneu grows wild and is believed to have survived the phylloxera crisis of the nineteenth century unscathed while all the cultivated wines died miserably on the vines. Yay, natives!

This indigenous grape was discovered twenty years earlier and subjected to cultivation and experimentation. Over those years, the company determined that the grape had good enological potential, which, translated, means it could make a damn fine wine. Along with Selma Blanca, also indigenous, Familia Torres is cultivating the Moneu in the Penedes region, around fifty kilometers west of Barcelona, where those species originally grew wild.

According to Miguel Jr., also known as Miguel Torres Maczassek, the Torres family is "gradually reviving the winegrowing heritage and richness of the Penedes and Catalonia."[57] To produce Selma Blanca and Moneu, the Torres family located almost fifty ancestral wine varietals, of which only six proved to have strong potential to make marketable wine. It would be lovely to see other countries and other wine businesses make similar efforts to make wine from native plants.

Perhaps the very best news for sustainably grown wine is that consumers wholeheartedly support it. According to Tim Carl, enthusiasm for "green wine"—that is, wine that is grown organically or otherwise sustainably—is on the rise. The body of consumers specifically interested in this sustainably produced product grew 500 percent from 2017 to 2021, and that trend is expected to continue. Carl notes, however, that the nebulous term *green wine* has no actual definition, guidelines, or governing body. As a result, winemakers can conduct some shady "greenwashing" if they choose to take a dirty shortcut.[58]

Some greenwashing consists of businesses simply using the word *green* to describe their processes. Such branding can be done with impunity because "green" can mean anything and everything, and there is no regulation about what that word can be applied to. Greenwashing could consist of reforming only a fraction of destructive practices, like leaving 10 percent of acreage untilled while heavily tilling the other 90 percent. Carl notes that the 2022 *Harvard Business Review* conducted a study of businesses claiming "green" practices. The study concluded that 42 percent of such claims are either inaccurate or exaggerated. Clearly, some universal certification is needed to provide consumers with the best information about what they are buying.[59]

What should vineyards and wineries do to mitigate the problems of climate change? There are at least a hundred things that wineries *could* do, but an exhaustive list is rarely helpful. But there are five imperative practices that the wine industry can and should implement, and many of the things on this list are not expensive, or they could save money over time.

1. Go organic, or at least reduce the use of pesticides. The days of preemptive chemical spraying should have been over and done with in the twentieth century. Grape-destroying pests can be discouraged through biocontrol—that is, introducing a predator who will minimize that pest's population. The best way to manage rodents is to encourage your native owls by putting up owl boxes. Dragonflies can be used to control other insect populations. The best way to biocontrol is to plant native florae that feed the predators you wish to encourage, but there are also specialists who can sell you dragonflies, ladybugs, praying mantises, and so on. Johnson-Bell also recommends a pheromone treatment to disrupt pest species reproduction.[60] When all else fails, and only when all else fails, pests should be treated with pesticides on a spot basis, not wholesale.
2. Conserve water. Water conservation can and should be executed on a number of levels. Irrigation is bad for wine grapes as well as the environment and should not be used every year, but only on an emergency basis. Rainwater harvest is the bare minimum any vineyard or winery should be doing. Gray water should be reused wherever it can be reused.
3. Reduce tillage. Machine tilling is, admittedly, an efficient way to kill weeds, but weeds can also be pulled by hand, by humans who need employment. A successful vineyard should be able to avoid re-tilling for years at a time. Leaving soil undisturbed makes it richer in nutrients that grapes need in order to mirror their unique terroir. In the United States, two federal programs help vineyards and other farms implement sustainable practices, especially no-till growing and water conservation and recycling. The Conservation Stewardship Program assists growers in implementing or improving sustainable farming practices, especially no-till growing. The Environmental Quality Incentives Program offers financial assistance as well as technical support to farms that protect natural resources, especially soil health and water conservation.
4. Reduce packaging, especially glass bottles. Ideally, every winery would have a bottle return program, offering five cents, as a wild estimate,

for every bottle that can be put back into circulation. Failing that, Johnson-Bell suggests a system of shipping wine in giant reusable containers and having them bottled regionally, where they can then be returned to the bottlers for reuse. As an alternative, she suggests designing lighter-weight bottles or even, horrors!, converting to light-weight plastic bottles.[61]

5. Plant native grapes! Native species will always need less water, less fertilizer, and fewer pesticides than exotic species. They will need to be replanted much less often because they won't die so easily. *Vitis vinifera* makes sense in the Mediterranean regions to which that species belongs. Why the rest of the world needs *Vitis vinifera* remains a mystery to me. The phrase "How dark the con of man" keeps popping into my mind. How did we all get conned into thinking we need European wines? The United States and Canada have multiple native grape species—including *Vitis aestivalis* and *Vitis rotundifolia*—that can be made into wine. Why have we given up on our native grapes?

What Can Wine Drinkers Do?

Wine drinkers of conscience must start voting with their dollars. The single best thing we can do is purchase wine that is made nearby. Instead of driving (contributing to climate change) to a grocery store and buying a French wine (that has contributed to climate change just by being on that shelf), get your nearby winery to ship you a few bottles. When we wine drinkers are on the road, perhaps going to or coming back from Christmas holidays or spring break, we should keep an eye out for wineries making local products. These are advertised right on the interstate, and you can also program Google Maps to tell you where all the independent wineries are on your route. These are good stopping points at which to stock up on wine. You need to first make sure that your local or regional winery is growing its own grapes, however, and not importing them from California.

Snobbery plays such a large part in wine purchases, but I'm not sure that the planet can survive that kind of snobbery. There is no empirical sense in which French wine is better than Missouri wine or Arkansas wine. Wine drinkers have, historically, bought into inherited assumptions far too often. Why is European wine better? Most people have no real answer to this question. We've been told it's better. We have been indoctrinated, and we need to un-indoctrinate ourselves.

We need to learn to like the wines that are made near to home. Part of a conscientious wine lover's activism should involve talking to local restaurants and wineshops about why they are not stocking local and regional wines—or at least wines made within five hundred miles of that store or restaurant. If a store or restaurant manager seems open to buying local vintages, arrange a meeting between the winemaker and the store, or at least make sure contact information is exchanged. If you hear that same thin line of bullshit—people don't like it, so I don't stock it—find a place to eat or shop that is more aligned with your values.

If you are part of a local or national environmental group, and you have regular meetings, hold those meetings in restaurants. As a group, you have more power than individual consumers. So, if you, as a group, put pressure on your local restaurants to buy organic and local products, they have to at least listen.

Wine lovers can also do the right thing by paying a little more money for organic products. Ideally, all our wines would be both local and organic, but if you have to drink wine that was grown a thousand miles away and shipped to your nearest Walgreens, at least honor the winemakers who are doing it right by buying the organic product. Wineries that are growing organically are most likely to also be employing other means of mitigating environmental damage, like rainwater conservation, use of alternative energy, and so on.

Should you make your own wine? It is not a terrible idea. With yeast, pectin, patience, and a little equipment, you can make wine or cider out of whatever is grown locally and in abundant supply. This saves you money and also reduces environmental impact.

Of course, wine drinkers should also recycle their wine bottles. Glass production, alone, is responsible for a surprising amount of air and water degradation. And glass recycling cuts back on the destruction of limited resources.

7
Must Wine Be Grape?

In a world gone mad enough to spray wine grapes with sunscreen, must wine come from grapes? I do realize it's heresy to ask this next question, but someone has to ask it: Should not California's and France's burning wine fields be turned over to making food while we explore more sustainable kinds of wine? Google "Why must wine be made of grapes?" and you will find contradictory answers. Grapes, posits *Atlas Obscura,* have the right amount of sugar and produce a product with a stable shelf life. Interestingly, the same article admits that "around the world, winemakers have killed themselves to grow grapes in places they really don't want to grow."[1] Other sources maintain that only grapes have the right level of acid, while yet others say that other fruits are too acidic and produce a wine that is too sharp tasting.

Most amusingly, *Wine Spectator* reports that grapes have skins and seeds that provide the tannins for a good wine.[2] Does *Wine Spectator* not realize that all fruits have seeds and skins? I ran over to the Tannin Food Intolerance website to confirm that all fruit is high in tannins, only to find that, no, oranges, lemons, and limes are not, though there are tannins in the skins of these foods.[3] Sure, that tracks. I haven't seen anyone trying to make wine from oranges. Yet.

According to Tannin Food Intolerance, some melons are also tannin-free, but not watermelon because of the seeds. And pineapple is tannin-free. I found that interesting in light of Hawaii's success in making an extremely popular wine from pineapple. Again, with the disclaimer: I am a lover and not an expert. But my palate tells me that cherries have pretty much the same levels of sweetness and tartness that grapes have, especially allowing that there are often extreme variations in sweetness from one berry to the next on the same tree or vine.

I'm tempted to draw an analogy between the insistence on grapes for wine and the Emperor's new clothes. Everyone can see that the Emperor is naked, just as everyone basically intuits that most fruit has sugar, acid, and tannins. But the charade continues because everyone is too much in awe of authority to point out the obvious. Grape wine, like the belief in god, needs a long history of followers willing to unthinkingly repeat some memorized verses, then get huffy when challenged with either science or experience.

As an antidote to superstition, let us consider the rice wine drunk all over Asia. Rice has a sugar content that is barely discernible to the average rice eater. Yet rice wine is *the* alcoholic drink in China, Japan, Thailand, Korea, and Vietnam. Basically, half the world gets its wine from a grain with very little inherent sweetness. And it is worth noting that rice wine is sweet, often nauseatingly so, to the Western palate. The popularity of rice as a wine base is pretty obviously all about the availability of rice. Rice is grown all over Asia. Rice is the great equalizer; it's eaten by the rich and the poor, and it makes a mean wine.

Rice wine is not my jam. The flagrant sweetness, lack of any tart or fruity notes, and phlegmy texture all repel me, but that doesn't mean it is not a good wine. It just means I don't like it. In sushi restaurants all over the Western world, the rice wine called sake gets the job done, and some people think that sushi just isn't sushi without rice wine. Let us consider the wild inconsistency of preferring a sweet, gloppy wine when eating sushi and then insisting that only dry wine is worth drinking when it's made with grapes. That glaring contradiction shines a definite light on wine snobbery in the United States and Europe.

When researching the dominance of the grape over all Western wines, I found that the specific way grape juice interacts with yeast is a more acceptable justification. And then there is the problem of shelf life. Wine made from grapes can be stabilized in bottles, where it lasts, potentially, for centuries. These bottles can be stored without refrigeration and even sent thousands of miles overseas. In the end, the great capacity of the grape, in winemaking, might come down to how it acts in a bottle. The least compelling argument is that grapes alone are sweet enough to make great wine.

Why are atheists (like me) scared to say they don't believe in god? It's the fear of popular opinion, right? All those churches, full of people talking to their imaginary friends. They have the weight of numbers combined with the hammer of tradition. Similarly, all those wine bars are filled with people who blindly accept that Cabernet is king, and Merlot is the spare heir. Ask them why good wine only comes from California or Europe, and they will say, "Everyone knows it. Any other wine is 'missing something.'" They have less evidence for their belief than the god botherers, but they have the numbers and the centuries of tradition.

I went to Elizabeth Schneider's book, *Wine for Normal People,* hoping to find some intelligent analysis of wine snobbery. Schneider, after all, has all the qualifications I lack. She is a sommelier with certification and holds a master's degree in business. She laments that "many people in the industry discourage you from learning yet put you down for not knowing stuff."[4] Her book's subtitle is *A Guide for Real People Who Like Wine, but Not the Snobbery That Goes with It.*

In her introduction, she writes about being a young woman working at a winery and being humiliated by the big boss. He caught her not knowing whether Dolcetto was a grape or a region and told her to hit the books. Schneider's response: "These lavish displays of schmuck-ery are everywhere in wine. The only thing you can do is walk away from these wine peacocks without losing it on them."[5]

Wine for Normal People is a good book with a beautiful, reader-friendly page design. From it, I learned that an overly dry wine lacking flavor can be called "tight" or "closed."[6] I also learned that the reason some people are so drawn to coffee *and* black tea *and* wine *and* dark chocolate, but not beer, lollipops, or Gatorade, is the tannins. Tea, coffee, baker's chocolate, and wine have tannins for days. But I searched in vain through *Wine for Normal People* for any hint that the wine snobbery Schneider deplores might extend to the notion that only grape wine is worth learning about.

According to Tasting Table, the best non-grape fruit wines are cherry wine from Michigan, peach wine from Colorado, pineapple wine from Hawaii, and apple wine from Connecticut. The article completely ignores the most obvious and historic non-grape wine—mead.[7]

Why Grapes? Why Not Honey?

The history of getting hammered starts with mead, an ancient drink made of fermented honey. And small wonder. At its most basic, the making of mead requires three ingredients: water, honey, yeast. Take that, twenty-first-century technology. No one ever needed you to get sweetly, gently buzzed.

Mead is such a low-tech drink that it occurs in nature with no help from humans. "The first time a beehive got flooded by rainwater, there was naturally occurring mead," Greg Heller-LaBelle, president of the American Mead Makers Association, is known to say.[8] And the formula for mead is surprisingly flexible. Some traditions call for equal parts honey and water, while others call for four parts water to one part honey or even more dilution.

If you want a science experiment that results in something more interesting than mold, you could ferment mead in one month using a sealed Home Depot bucket and ingredients you bought at the grocery section of Walmart.

An article on the website for Penn Museum notes that "the earliest chemically confirmed alcoholic beverage in the world was at Jiahu in the Yellow River Valley of China (Henan province), ca. 7000–6600 B.C. (Early Neolithic Period). It was an extreme fermented beverage made of wild grapes (the earliest attested use), hawthorn, rice, and honey."[9]

According to both Jewish and Islamic traditions as well as those of Ethiopia's Christian orthodoxy, the Queen of Sheba served mead to King Solomon during their first, very important meeting. If Sheba truly existed, she probably hailed from Yemen or Ethiopia. Unfortunately, there's little to no archeological evidence for her. But, you know, if you believe it, it's religion; if you don't believe it, it's mythology.

In Louisville, Kentucky, the best Ethiopian restaurant is the Queen of Sheba, and that fine institution formerly represented mead as inextricably bound up in Ethiopian culture and history. You could not be seated without seeing some kind of serious literature about the Bible and honey wine. This is religion, not mythology. Queen of Sheba (the restaurant) proudly offered a traditional mead, made in Ethiopia, called tej, or t'ej. The distinctive of tej is that, in addition to the water, honey, and yeast, the Ethiopians add gesho leaves. The gesho is a subspecies of the buckthorn shrub, and the result is an ever-so-light-handed hoppy or beer-y taste.

According to Kristina Gratzer and several of her colleagues, Ethiopia today has six million beehives. Eighty percent of the honey derived from those hives goes to making mead.[10] Ethiopians are serious about their mead; it is not a novelty item as in other parts of the world. Mead turns up in the *Rig-Veda* around 1100 BCE. Conveniently for the god Vishnu, mead popped up in springs where he set his godly feet. Drinking from this holy spring boosted fertility, especially the likelihood of making boy babies.

The Homeric Greeks and their ancient contemporaries among the Egyptians, Romans, and Phoenicians definitely drank mead, and their poets referenced it frequently in their heroic ballads. Mead provided courage in advance of a battle and celebratory sedation in the event that your team won. It also liberated the soul from the bonds of cold sobriety and was, therefore, a spiritual lubricant.

The god of wine—Bacchus to the Romans, Dionysius to the Greeks—was technically the god of mead before he became posh and took up grape wine. Some scholars believe that the nectar of the gods was, indeed, nothing other than wine made from honey. Thereafter, mead soon appears as the main social lubricant of those wild European Northmen. Mead softens cold Nordic hearts in *Beowulf*, the *Nibelungenlied*, and the Icelandic sagas.

Citizens of the Roman Empire were accomplished beekeepers, none too dependent on finding a wild hive in the woods. They trimmed logs and wove baskets to colonize bees and keep them happily making honey. Honey, for this advanced civilization, was both an ingredient for booze and a delicious sweetener for desserts like honey cakes. At the height of the Roman Empire, its leaders considered mead an inferior drink, and they preferred wine made from grapes. Therefore, the tables of Rome city would feature grape wine during meals, with mead possibly served as an aperitif or dessert. But, according to mead expert Fred Minnick, outside Rome, the rest of the empire drank mead.[11] It was cheaper, easier to make, and more available to the farmers and road builders of that vast empire.

The voice of the Roman mead drinkers was a soldier and farmer turned writer named Lucius Junius Moderatus Columella. Columella, as he is called for short, lived in the first century AD. He wrote fourteen books that today we might call "cookbooks." He was the Betty Crocker of his time, making sure to cover all the culinary bases. In Columella, we can see civilization pivoting away from mead to grape-based wine. Though he devoted a few passages to mead making, Columella spent more energy teaching folks how to make grape wine. His best mead recipe calls for the addition of several fruits: pomegranate, quince, apples, and grapes. This mixture of mead with wine fruits is called "pyment," and it foreshadowed the kind of trendy hybrid meads that winemakers are brewing today.

But Columella also provided a simple mead recipe that reverted back to the traditional ingredients, water, honey, and time. After leaving the rainwater and honey to mix in the sun for forty days, you seasoned Columella's mead by exposing it to a room with smoke. This brew, he noted, could be added to livestock feed to make chickens and oxen fatter and juicier. Mead, Columella added, can also be used as the basis for sauces and even cucumber brine, if you want sweet pickles.[12]

In Russia, Vladimir the Great was a dedicated mead drinker, among many other things. He ordered three hundred vats of mead at one time to celebrate a battle he won. Vladimir the Great is perhaps best known for ousting paganism en masse from his territories. He accomplished this by ordering his people to be baptized into Christianity or be his enemy. As in most mass conversions, the death threat was thinly veiled. Minnick hints that, after their baptism in the river, Vladimir's constituents celebrated with a flagon of weak mead.[13] As a likely outcome of Vladimir's mead predilection, the state of Novgorod became a major mead-making region. Some Russians mixed their mead with raspberries to get a specific tart, fruity result. Beyond that, Russian mead came in red or white. The white mead was processed with river water and beer yeast, yielding a more hoppy concoction. The red mead was mixed with berries, cinnamon, cloves, and fish gelatin.

Mead was frequently drunk out of giant ladles, which certainly simplified the pouring process. With a ladle, your pitcher and wineglass are one. This might seem barbaric until one realizes that, among the wealthier Russians, one of these ladles, called a kovsh, could be made out of silver or gold. These implements were so lavish that they made good gifts to out-of-town guests. London's Victoria and Albert Museum houses one that was gifted to Don Cossack Timothy Turaberin by Empress Anna Ioannovna.

According to Minnick, Russia's 1654 tax on mead put it in competition with vodka and beer at festivals. Slowly, but inexorably, mead was edged out by the other beverages, and by 1840, mead was the refuge of drinkers with little money.[14] "With so many ancient connections to this historic drink, it's clear that Russia, a land known for its vodka cravings, was originally a mead state, with honey second only to wheat in agricultural harvesting and beekeepers farming honey just for mead," Minnick writes.[15]

No history of mead would be complete without a dip into medieval Poland. Prince Leszek the White accepted Christianity and promoted it throughout eastern Europe. But when Pope Innocent III called on him to send soldiers on a crusade that would retake Jerusalem, Leszek famously declined, explaining that "neither he nor any self-respecting Polish knight could be induced to go to the Holy Land, where, they had been informed, there was no wine, mead, or even beer to be had."[16] Clearly, in this instance, mead was superior to beer. Imagine. No beer. And you call that land holy?

The Slavs and Goths who lived in Poland were also quite fond of mead and used it to jack themselves up for war and then calm themselves down afterward. Mead, in fact, remained a highly sought resource in Poland after other parts of Europe and Asia had converted to grape wine drinking. As late as the fifteenth century, the Polish duke Janusz III ordained that mead would be available only to the upper classes.[17]

For hundreds of years, in other words, wine was made from honey. When wine historians write about the origins of wine, they often skip over mead as if it is of no account. If you entirely dismiss mead culture, which seems a little arbitrary considering that mead is made using the same basic processes as grape wine, then the first purely grape wine can be traced to Georgia. That's the eastern European country of Georgia, not the state of the union, of course. Artifacts related to Georgian wine date its origins to around 6000 BCE. Even after grape wine, that upstart, made its appearance, mead stood its own for years, often served at the same table whenever and wherever revelry was afoot.

Over time, though, wine made from grapes, and that nouveau wildcatter, beer, elbowed mead off the table and out of the taverns. And not for any particularly good reason that historians or wine experts have identified. In the second decade of the twenty-first century, though, mead has enjoyed an unexpected resurgence in popularity. It has popped up on the menus of some of the hottest new restaurants and bars. *Meadery* is a word that has reentered modern English with ferocity. Around every major metropolis, there are at least one or two meaderies. Google Maps shows at least four of them near downtown Chicago.

It has taken mead hundreds of years to make this comeback. At least three of my sources suggest the influence of HBO's wildly successful television show *Game of Thrones,* in which Tywin Lannister and other characters neck back mead out of their steins and glasses. "If you want to credit Game of Thrones, in which characters enjoy a ceremonial horn of mead, the timing works out—the show first aired in April 2011, when the number of commercial meaderies operating in the United States was shy of 200. Today, there are at least 480," writes Chris Klimek for *Smithsonian Magazine.*[18] Okay, maybe the show *got* people to try mead, but surely the taste is what generated the loyal and growing mead following. And there is just the faintest possibility that the young adults who are creating a market demand for mead have some sense of responsibility about the ecological impact of what they eat and drink. Let us pray.

One of the leaders in this surge is Jason Phelps, who has opened up a meadery in Manchester, New Hampshire. According to Phelps, the wine industry has remained static through a shift in tastes, a shift in favor of the sweet and spicy.[19] Mead satisfies that dark need to get a little buzzed on something sweet while also providing a break from the same old. At his meadery, Phelps blends fermented honey, without which a drink cannot truly call itself "mead," with spices, herbs, fruit, and even hops. This freehanded blending is typical of the new meaderies, and it explains why mead, technically a wine, is usually marketed alongside beers, especially craft beers.

In my humble opinion, mead and other agricultural products could replace about half the world's grape wine without any quantitative loss in human happiness. The main argument for mead replacing grape wine is the potential sustainability of mead. Unlike wine grapes, honey can be farmed intensively with less land, less water, and altogether less stress on the natural world. Honey can also be farmed—well, maybe not everywhere, but certainly in more places than one can grow wine grapes. Honey not only can but must be produced without the use of pesticides, making mead inherently better for shared air, soil, and water.

One or two meaderies could potentially supply most of the wine needs of a medium-sized town, and if people bought their local mead, they would be avoiding the climate costs of transporting wine to the Midwest from California, France, South Africa, Chile, and Israel. Of course, people could also support their regional wineries and buy wine grown and made there. But, again, snobbery and the insane belief that only in a few places, not here, can good wine be made prevail. Ken Schramm, who has been making mead for thirty-five years in Michigan, says that "mead is perhaps headed to be the drink that, if it's made as it can be and stays in its own environment, can be the lowest carbon-footprint beverage there is."[20]

Brett and Megan Hines came to the same conclusion. When they started up their organic farm in Maryland, they wanted to make an alcoholic brew of some kind. They had already learned the art of making craft beer. But making beer requires huge supplies of barley and hops. And these mostly have to be shipped from Washington State, Idaho, North Dakota, Montana, and other western states. "We wanted to make a truly local beverage. And a lot of grain is grown far away at a big commercial scale. Bringing grain in from across the country is not a sustainable long-term thing," Megan tells the *Washington Post*.[21] So instead of transporting grain, they raised bees, and they now sell their mead at their very own Buzz Meadery, located in Berlin, Maryland.

Mead maker Ayla Guild of Wisconsin notes that, even in a drought, bees are "scrappy" and will find food sources. "Certain plants thrive in drought, and the bees know how to find them," Guild tells the *Washington Post*. That means that no mead maker has to irrigate to keep their crop alive.[22]

At the risk of sounding like mead is the answer to every prayer, there is yet another reason that mead rocks. Bees are in trouble, with hives disappearing, and bee populations are in mysterious decline. Pesticides do their part to kill bees, but the people who won't give up their killing sprays point to the varroa mite, which attacks bee colonies. In the United States, the varroa is an invasive species that showed up around 1987 and began devastating bees both in the wild and in managed hives.

According to the Associated Press, half of the honeybee hives in the United States died in 2022, leaving beekeepers the last best hope for keeping this important pollinator from extinction.[23] Small-scale beekeepers have traditionally made little money from selling honey; what money is to be made is largely from "renting" bees to large farms because there is no actual substitute for insect pollinators. But there is a strong revenue model for making alcoholic beverages. Therefore, beekeepers can actually earn a stable income by supplying mead makers or by making their own craft mead. Greg Fischer, who manages Wild Blossom, a Chicago meadery, also produces his own honey from a hundred hives that he maintains in the Chicago area. "Bees are super important to the environment," Fischer says. "And right now, beekeepers are the ones that are keeping them alive."[24]

Apples

In 1999, I was honeymooning in Frankfurt, Germany, with Joel Parker Worth III, my best friend and the love of my life. Frankfurt had never been on the list of cities I desperately needed to see, but our flight landed us there. So it only made sense to spend a couple of days exploring. What we discovered was a perfectly lovely city, not as wild and imaginative as Berlin of the '90s, but a near-utopian midsize city, clean as a whistle and lavishly decorated with flower boxes. By a lovely coincidence, we arrived during the city's Apfelwein festival.

It was not exactly my first apple wine. I had spent a few days in Germany as a rising college junior, and predictably, men paid attention to me. My friend Marianne, with whom I was traveling, and I were treated to glasses of apple wine, which we drank politely while wishing it were sweeter. I had, at that time, no palate for wine, beer, or any other refreshing adult beverage. But, as an older and wiser honeymooner in Frankfurt, I found the wine quite interesting. It's very different from cider, not as crisp or tart, but featuring the complexity that one finds in a fine grape wine.

The main difference between cider and apple wine is the level of carbonation. True apple wine is processed in a manner that allows the air to escape, resulting in a smooth, lush drink—well, you know, wine. By contrast, the cider process sequesters the air and turns it into bubbles. Apple wine is also more translucent than its cider cousin, which tends to be cloudy, dark, or amber.

You might find a bottle of Apfelwein in a resort wineshop, probably at a ski lodge. But mostly the Germans keep it for themselves, scarfing down the lion's share of it in the late fall and early winter, then transferring loyalty to a Riesling in the new year, and not worrying about whether either of these products is cool enough to be seen on their tables.

Apfelwein, as they call apple wine in German, is an acquired taste, just as is any wine or beer, blue cheese, or dark chocolate. I could tell that I would come to like it, if I drank it two or three more times. So Joel and I sat outdoors on a perfect, clear and mild May day near the tables where Apfelwein was being marketed and enjoyed the wee buzz that fermented apples bring to the human brain. We felt tolerated, if not outright welcome, in that city at that time. Americans were not yet blamed for spreading terrorism or COVID-19. It was a great time to travel.

I wouldn't get to try another Apfelwein until, many years later, I found a bottle of it at a wine boutique in north Georgia. The store had such an eclectic selection that I couldn't help asking a sales associate if they had not considered carrying a Cynthiana. She told me that the owner handpicks every brand and every bottle and that she has very specific tastes. The apple wine actually lived up to that kind of praise. I knew I would like it if I met it again.

The history of mead and its recent comeback raises a question that cannot be ignored: Why is grape wine so popular in the Western world, while wine made with other fruits is regarded as a rather silly novelty? In my day, if one mentioned "fruit wine" (as if grapes are anything but fruit), someone would invariably invoke the name of Boone's Farm. As a graduate student, I had never actually tried Boone's Farm, but the uncoolness of it was enough to keep me buying cheap, atrocious Chablis wherever a grad school party popped up. This, despite the fact that the Germans make a sturdy, indisputably delicious wine out of apples.

So why is there so little apple wine in the United States? We have apples in bushels; in truckloads; in the poetry of Robert Frost, Stephen Vincent Benet, and Vachel Lindsay. But so, so little wine from apples. It wasn't always this way. The dream of Johnny Appleseed was that every homeowner in America would have his own apple orchard, his own wine/cider press, and his own home brew. For most pioneers, that home brew would be apple cider. Appleseed, whose real name was Jonathan Chapman, traveled the midwestern United States in advance of major settlements. The Ohio Company of Associates, a land company, granted a hundred free acres to settlers who pushed the boundary of the western frontier. *But* those settlers had to plant fifty apple trees and twenty peach trees within their first three years of settlement.

This was something of a hardship because fruit trees do not immediately produce a product that can be sold or consumed. But planting fruit trees was symbolic of a determination to stick it out in disputed territory over which Native Americans were still fighting with the encroachers. So Chapman carried his leather bag full of seeds all over Ohio, Illinois, Indiana, Ontario, and parts of West Virginia. He planted orchards, which he fenced in to prevent predation, then moved on. Years later, he would circle back to an orchard he had planted and sell the trees to a new settler who then had a leg up on the rules.

Chapman's practice of growing apples from seeds was eccentric. The only way to ensure a tree produces edible apples is with grafting. But Chapman was a Swedenborgian; in that sect, grafting is frowned on because it injures the plant. Most of the trees that Chapman planted produced sour or bitter apples, not good for the table, but great for making cider and apple cider vinegar, which is a *great* flavor maker and marinade, particularly valuable to people trying to build a meal around a dead squirrel or opossum. Cider vinegar also has possible health benefits—lowering blood sugar, helping with weight management—which naturopaths are still exploring.

Chapman biographer William Kerrigan suggests another reason that cider, rather than beer, was so popular among the Midwest's settlers: to make beer, the farmers would have to dedicate serious farmland to raising grain. But they needed to produce food and cash crops with that land.[25] By contrast, an apple tree is a mostly vertical enterprise, and one mature tree could produce enough apples to make cider for the whole family.

The typical cider of the early Midwest was a weak brew that could be imbibed daily and was often drunk as a safer alternative to water. Of course, this raises the thorny problem of dehydration, about which I have been worrying for a while. If the pioneers drank a lot of cider or beer instead of water, how did that not kill them?

The internet hive mind generally agrees that a beverage that is 2 percent alcohol or less is hydrating, while "regular beer" with a 5 percent alcohol content is hydration neutral. At least two studies strongly suggest that a moderate amount of 5 percent beer after a workout neither hydrates nor dehydrates the drinker.[26] (There is a current trend among some athletes of drinking nonalcoholic beer as part of recovery from extreme exertion. Nonalcoholic beer has half a percent of alcohol, which is the equivalent amount of alcohol you would get from eating a banana.)

This research suggests that the healthiest pioneers would have pressed and consumed cider that was consistently less than 5 percent alcohol. They could drink that all day and not get heatstroke. In the winter, a 3 or 4 percent cider might act like an extra pair of long underwear. And such a beverage would have an electrolyte content similar to Gatorade. In other words, it would fight fatigue.

If a pioneer wanted to get good and trashed, he needed to press and ferment applejack, an early American whisky made entirely of those mostly inedible home-farmed apples. Though applejack has mostly faded from the collective American consciousness, it was a respectable drink among our founding fathers. Robert Laird was the chief commercial producer of applejack during George Washington's life, and a letter exists in which Washington asks Laird for the recipe. FDR liked him some applejack in his Manhattans. And, as late as 1967, LBJ gifted a case of applejack to Soviet statesman and policymaker Alexei Nikolayevich Kosygin to take the chill off the Cold War.[27]

Chapman had to be well aware that he was planting for cider and applejack, not for the apple a day that keeps the doctor away. And there were good health reasons for pressing cider. Water was easily contaminated; the fermenting process banished unwholesome bacteria. Most frontier ciders were half as alcoholic as a typical wine, and cider is packed with antioxidants. Some writers have portrayed Chapman as more opportunist than philanthropist. He did not give trees away; he sold them, and it was an iron-clad revenue stream. When he died, his sister inherited a wealth of unsold trees, but the estate was soon badly reduced by taxes and legal fees.

Even though Chapman did not run a nonprofit, he lived humbly, dressed simply, often going barefoot, and accepting whatever hospitality was on offer, there at the outer edge of civilization. He must have enjoyed his own company more than most. But he was also good company to the many people who hosted him. These included even the Native Americans whom the Europeans were displacing. Chapman was particularly good with children. For their amusement, he would stick straight pins into his feet and even walk on hot coals, suggesting an unusually high pain threshold.

According to some historians, Chapman was kicked in the head by a horse when he was young. His skull was fractured, and a piece of his skull was surgically removed to alleviate pressure on his brain. This practice was called "trepanning." Whether this injury occurred, in fact, is debatable, but many history scholars need an explanation for Chapman's eccentricities. We know that he was not cognitively impaired, however, because he would give dramatic readings to his hosts out of the sacred texts of Emanuel Swedenborg.

Chapman was a vegetarian, though the teachings of Swedenborg do not definitely require his followers to abstain from meat. This meat abstinence must have been a hardship: Chapman walked long distances and would have needed protein. In the undeveloped Midwest, it was a lot easier to get your protein by shooting a deer than by growing fifty potatoes. In alignment with vegetarianism, he was a friend to animals and insects. Howard Means writes, "Gentle as a lamb, he became a legendary figure in a land ruled by gun, knife, and fist. . . . In dress and diet, he calls most directly to mind another voice in the wilderness: John the Baptist, with his camel hair cloak and meals of locusts and wild honey. Yet unlike that John, there was nothing fierce about this one."[28]

Chapman never married, trusting that the afterlife would provide him with a bride. To say he was not generous with his time and energy would be a little cynical. He definitely had a vision, and that vision was a country filled with apples and settlers who would never lack the comfort of a mildly sedating cider. "Really, what Johnny Appleseed was doing and the reason he was welcome in every cabin in Ohio and Indiana was he was bringing the gift of alcohol to the frontier. He was our American Dionysus," says Michael Pollan.[29]

During Prohibition, the FBI chopped down many apple trees, suspected of growing cider apples.[30] America's DIY cider culture toppled with them. But Americans still see apples as a symbol of our identity. When we say something is as "American as apple pie," we could, just as easily, be saying "American as apple wine or cider."

Apple wine culture was not lost during Prohibition, though. It pivoted. In 1961, Ernest and Julio Gallo started producing cheap apple wine for people whose wine budgets did not stretch to the more prestigious California or European vintages. And, you guessed it, this apple wine was distributed under E. & J.'s Boone's Farm label. Strawberry Hill, another Boone's Farm vintage, was also an apple wine with strawberry flavoring added. Also added were the echoes of Louis Armstrong's "Blueberry Hill" and the thrill he found there.

Boone's Farm was but one affordable alcoholic beverage in the Ernest and Julio Gallo constellation. These brothers, third-generation Italian Americans, started up their empire just as Prohibition was ending. Their timing was perfect. There was a deficit of wine grape production, but their father, Joseph Edward Gallo Sr., had bought a great deal of farmland in California and had been growing grapes and shipping them across the country for home use at a time when Americans were allowed to make wine at home but could not buy it at a store.

In 1933, the same year that Prohibition ended, Joseph Edward Gallo, the patriarch, shot his wife and then killed himself. As the new head of the family, Joseph's son Ernest famously declared that he wanted the Gallo wine business to be the "Campbell's soup company of the wine industry." What he wanted, in other words, was for Gallo to be a household name with products that everyone could afford. White Port and Thunderbird, wines fortified up to 20 percent alcohol, were marketed to the inner city.[31]

By contrast, the Boone's Farm line offered softer, milder drinks. In 1972, Mark Singer wrote an article for *Esquire* titled "Sweet Wine of Youth," in which he explored the young Americans' love of "pop wine." When Singer used the term *pop wine,* he meant Boone's Farm apple wines and other fruity, sweet, super affordable vintages. "Boone's Farm Apple Wine, the current leader among all pop wines, retails for up to $1.10 per fifth, depending upon local taxes and the shipping distance from the E. & J. Gallo Co. Winery in Modesto, California," he wrote.[32]

Where and how did these wholesome young Americans develop a taste for cheap wine? Singer and other writers of that age believed that U.S. military men discovered wine while stationed overseas and that young Americans backpacking through Europe developed a taste for cheap Burgundy and other *Vitis vinifera* varietals. When those same backpackers got home, though, they discovered that Burgundy in U.S. stores was far too expensive, so they transitioned to Boone's Farm or something similarly cheap.

Singer predicted the teens and college undergraduates who were enjoying these sweet, cheap apple wines would, over time, graduate to more sophisticated vintages as their tastes improved and their wallets fattened. Would they have had to graduate to grape wine, or could they not have demanded better apple wines? We may never know because apple wine was effectively driven from our shores by the 1991 congressional tax hike on wine. In a 1990 article titled "Taxing Vices," the *Washington Post* reported that the tax on beer would double, the tax on liquor would get a very small adjustment, and the tax on wine would go up 700 percent. It doesn't take higher math to see that this was bad, bad news for the wine drinkers.[33]

Under this new schedule, it no longer made sense for Ernest and Julio to continue making cheap apple wine. So they didn't. The Boone's Farm label would continue to thrive, but a bottle of Boone's would not contain wine; it would contain a malt product, much like Mike's Hard Lemonade or Zima.

Consumers were no longer getting apple wine; they were getting strawberry-flavored beer or apple-flavored beer. Malt beverages, you see, were taxed as beer, not as wine. Boone's Farm would no longer be a ladder to better wines; it would be a ladder straight to cheap rum and vodka or really anything that tastes better than a malt beverage. And that's a big tent.

Interesting, because Boone's Farm wine, in its original formula, was never that alcoholic. While parents wrung their hands over the mere thought of their teens in the woods with a bottle of sweet wine, Boone's Strawberry Hill was 9 percent alcohol, according to Singer's 1972 article. Boone's had a solid reputation for causing crazy behavior and bad hangovers. But only very inexperienced drinkers could have achieved that result on Boone's Farm alone. That's why it was so often paired with cannabis. We might also have to admit that teenagers are just capable of making bad decisions, whether drunk or sober.

Recipes and tax laws have changed over the decades since the 1991 changes. Today, Boone's Farm's most popular drink is the Blue Hawaiian, typically found on the bottom shelf of a convenience store. The ingredients list is a horror show of carbonated water, dextrose, and fructose. Underneath the natural flavors, there's an admission that it contains an undisclosed quantity of apple wine. Then follow the potassium citrate, potassium sorbate, sorbitol, gum acacia, medium chain triglycerides, sucrose acetate isobutyrate, sulfiting agents, and, of course, blue food coloring, because you could not possibly expect that bright lagoon blue to arise naturally out of the other ingredients. Writing for Mashed, Crawford Smith pretty much sums up the typical adult reaction to Blue Hawaiian: "Curious, you buy a bottle, bring it home, take a taste, and wonder how something so intensely sweet and downright syrupy could be called wine."[34]

By far the most amusing thing about Blue Hawaiian is its 3 percent alcohol content. The high school and college (?) students who drink it have to either drink Herculean quantities or use their imaginations about what being drunk feels like. The combination of nonnutritive, calorific ingredients with a blue color not occurring in nature and low, low alcohol content make Blue Hawaiian empirically one of the worst values I can imagine. Has apple wine been kicked to the curb, the curb being a bottom-shelf alcoholic Gatorade, with little to no appeal for anyone over nineteen? As it turns out, no, America's apple culture is still thriving. The use of apples in bottom-shelf college swill is only one facet of America's infatuation with apples. The cider industry is thriving alongside craft beer and microbreweries. Beer and cider are often produced side by side by the same companies.

Nor has apple wine been lost. Apple wineries crop up all over the United States, and some are quite upscale. The rule of thumb seems to be that the pricier a tourist destination is, the more gourmet the apple wine. New York State has, arguably, the most upscale apple wineries. Most of these boast that the apples are grown right there on the estate. Apple Station Winery in Cayuga is a typical destination winery offering space for banquets, showers, meetings, weddings, and so on. Family owned, the winery has its own apple orchard from which it presses apple wine, cider, other fruit wines, apple gin, and apple vodka. In spring, summer, and fall, visitors are welcomed to the tasting room, and they are free to walk among the apple trees and even enjoy the company of the resident livestock: goats, chickens, and sheep.

Google "apple wine" and you will also find a hefty subculture of people offering recipes and DIY tips for the home brewer. You will find people posting questions about making apple wine at home. Apple wine exists in the United States as a craft project. I looked at a few internet recipes but got scared off the project because the directions varied so wildly from one food writer to the next. Often, I got the impression that the writer didn't know wine basics. One very confident recipe writer said to add a "bit of sugar" for "sweetness" instead of pointing out that sugar is a major determiner of alcohol content.

But the main reason I won't be making apple wine any time soon is the amount of time it takes to age it. One site estimated six weeks to six months after an initial fermentation of ten days. I immediately recognized that I am simply not patient enough to be a winemaker. Either I'm going to be drinking apple juice and spiking it with brandy or someone's going to unearth my apple wine vats while clearing out the house after my death. At that point, my heirs will have discerned that I forgot all about my passion for apple wine and moved on to other enthusiasms.

While writing this book, I stumbled on a sort of apple mall in the mountains of north Georgia. Mercier Orchards, in Blue Ridge, looks like a modest establishment from the road. When I got inside, I realized it was the size of a TJ Maxx. This is where apple lovers go to find anything relevant to the fruit. It is organized like a department store, with wines in one corner, raw apples in the center, pastries in another section, jams and jellies occupying their own wall, apple artwork, kitchen supplies, and so on. Customers are encouraged to pick up a grocery cart on entering. And if one gets fatigued in the process of loading up on apple products for the year, there is a café with indoor and outdoor seating, as well as a bar for bored husbands/fathers. I was enormously grateful to see that they also sold locally made wines, including Fat Boy and another Cynthiana-based wine, called Blood Mountain, from Three Sisters.

The Mercier website mentions that you can pick your own fruit or take a tractor ride through the fields. It also features a downloadable guide to caring for and preserving your apples, which I greatly appreciated. Really, food preservation should be taught in schools as a required, core subject. But, in the absence of that, it's nice to see businesses picking up the slack.

One could easily spend $1,000 in the Mercier store. I opted for a wine tasting. There were several apple wines on offer, and I left with a bottle. I also purchased a bottle of Blood Mountain, two bottles of Fat Boy, and a single jug of unfiltered apple juice to which shots of brandy were surreptitiously added back home.

In searching for an apple winemaker closer to Louisville, I remembered Huber's Orchard and Winery. Huber's is one of two local wineries that have successfully marketed to package stores across the income brackets. I can find a bottle of Huber's fruit wine at the very nice grocery a half mile away and also at J. R. Liquors, a store within walking distance of my house that strives to manage its low-income loiterers. Huber's has somehow managed to appeal to everyone.

So I have to confess to having sampled Huber's wines and found them overly sweet and simplistic. In general, I prefer dry reds that pair well with plant food, cheese, eggs, and fish. Table wines, to use the most prosaic prose. But Huber's has apple wine, and it was only a forty-minute drive, so Joel drove me there on a Saturday. According to local news sources, the Huber family has been growing fruit in southern Indiana since 1843. Huber's you-pick business is believed to be the first of its kind in the state. Their seven hundred acres are in the small town of Starlight, Indiana.

On Google Maps, Huber's looks a fraction of a mile off the interstate. As we were making the eighth turn and getting farther and farther into the rural parts of the Ohio River Valley, Joel said, "I thought this was right off the highway."

"Hey, we haven't seen any peacocks yet; calm down," I told him. As we pulled into the driveway and saw about five hundred parked cars, I realized it was a mistake to come here on a Saturday in autumn. Huber's isn't an orchard. It's like Disney World and the county fair got together and made a baby. Several hundred people were milling around under tents, making purchases. There were food trucks and several permanent structures, one specializing in sales of ice cream and cheese. A few people who wanted some alone time had gone down to the bank of a pond and were feeding ducks. There were several different ticket lines and several outbuildings, including a restaurant.

I felt overwhelmed. We lucked out, finding a parking space within five minutes. But the throngs of humanity unnerved me a little. Any time I find myself around that many people, I feel like I might have done something wrong. This is probably why I've never been to Disney. We waited in line to get directions to the right line, then waited in line for tickets. Then we took our tickets upstairs and waited in line for our wine and spirits tastings for about twenty minutes. Again, I was reminded why I've never gone to Six Flags.

The decor in the wine tasting room was decidedly Americana, with a raised, barn-like ceiling and middle-American, mid-last-century decor, including what looked like a Shell gasoline pump from the 1950s. Our sommelier was having a rough day, and his hands shook. I thought about recommending the medication I take for my own tremor, but Joel assured me it would be wildly inappropriate.

Whenever I see someone around my age working in the service industry, I am dying to know the story. Are they bored? Are they fighting dementia and loneliness? Did they blow all their savings on a sick child or grandchild? Are they using this job as a bully pulpit to get their strongly held political messages out there? Do they need to insure a younger wife or husband? Those aren't wild-hair examples, by the way. I've met all those people. I may very well be one of those people, at some point. Then I remembered that Huber's has a strong mission for employing veterans. His tremor might well be PTSD, as mine is.

The spiced apple, which seems to be Huber's signature wine, was fairly predictable. It would pair well with cheddar and/or a pork chop and some chive potatoes. It was not layered like an Apfelwein can be. There was a Vignoles on the menu, so I ordered that, and it took me straight back to Missouri and the huge surprise of discovering that delightful and mostly American vintage. This one was not so forward with the pineapple, but it perked me up with its crisp, off-dry fruity flavor. Vignoles continues to amaze me with its murky history, mysterious origins, and bright, hopeful, dare I say, somewhat American taste. I generally hate white wines and, truth be told, only order them when I want to drop some pounds, white wine packing fewer calories than red.

I'm having to rethink my entire wine experience here. Do I like sweet whites and just don't want to admit it? No, no, I hate Moscato and Riesling. I was able to drink Blue Nun in college but would not now touch it with another wine drinker's hands. I also hate Chablis and Pinot Grigio and can barely tolerate Chardonnay, so that pretty much covers the dry whites.

Might it be that I actually have a taste for the semisweet whites? To test this theory, I ordered the Traminette, also described as a semisweet white. Traminette was developed in the laboratories of the University of Illinois and Cornell. Herb C. Barrett developed it around 1965 to imitate the German Gewürztraminer to an extent. As a wine that started in a lab, it was also bred to be hardy, cold resistant, and slow to catch diseases. It was named the signature wine of Indiana, which is fitting because Huber's is an Indiana winery. It wasn't quite as delicious as the Vignoles, but still more drinkable than other whites. Maybe this semisweet variety is the white for me.

The Huber's experience was all good news. Though I don't like crowds, it was uplifting to see that many people getting some version of America's legacy apple culture. Google Maps took us back home along a new set of back roads, and we saw acres and acres of grapevines, stretching for miles through southern Indiana. I've assumed most or all of these belong to Huber's Orchard. Wine, after all, is their real business, while the orchard experience offers employment to many locals and education to visiting families.

So America's apple culture has not been kicked to the curb, but it has shifted into something a little like theme parks. These orchard destinations combine wineries with apple picking, wedding venues, and even what I would call petting zoos. It does matter that we still have a strong, though not highly visible, apple culture. Apples have the virtue of growing almost everywhere in the United States, and growing them is substantially less challenging and less taxing on natural resources than growing grapes, especially European wine grapes.

For people who think about their carbon footprint, local, affordable apple wines would be a godsend. The locavore movement encourages consumers to get most or all of their food from within a radius of a hundred miles or so. Like wine, locavorism is multilayered. Many proponents believe that the taste and nutrition of their food will be higher if they eat products grown nearby.

Beyond that, locavorism supports small-scale growers who are more likely to employ sustainable growing practices, practices that do not deplete soil and water. Supporting organic farmers and other small, sustainable growers puts pressure on corporate farms to reduce their use of pesticides and chemical fertilizers, reducing agricultural pollution.

The concerns of locavores intersect with the concerns of climate change advocates who understand that transportation is the biggest contributor to planetary warming, fiercer storms, and droughts. While reducing one's own use of gasoline by driving less or owning an electric car goes a distance, the thoughtful locavore or climate advocate must also consider the ecological costs of food that is transported hundreds of miles to the consumer.

Cherries

If we are going to talk about the sugar content of fruit in relation to its eligibility to make wine, we must acknowledge that ripe cherries are just as sweet as grapes. It's baffling that cherry wine, even when so affirmatively endorsed by Prince, has not had its full day in the bright footlights of celebrity. The unhipness of cherry wine is not stopping cherry growers in Door County, Wisconsin, and all over Michigan from producing some great wine, however.

Admittedly, the enjoyment of any particular wine is often—if not always—about context. A ten-dollar bottle of wine paired with some government cheese—lovingly laid out on a table and consumed with someone you feel affection for, with lots of eye contact, emotional affirmation, and occasional touching—might well be more memorable than a thousand-dollar bottle of Chateau Lafite shared with someone who bores you.

The weekend I spent in Door County was the former. Reunited with my beautiful husband after eight weeks apart, I was in the frame of mind to think that life was beautiful, and the world was new. The August weather was perfect. Everywhere we went, there was a view of Lake Michigan. Boats, harbors, green verges, and that everlasting symbol of monied leisure: the wineries.

The cherry wines were surprising. I was expecting a middling concoction that resembled Kool-Aid more than actual wine. I was wrong. Like grapes, cherries can be manipulated in the winemaking process to be sweet, dry, or somewhere in between. Like dry grape wine, dry cherry wine is layered and goes down well with food.

Michigan is the undisputed mother of cherry wine. Bing cherries are liable to produce a sweet cherry wine, but black cherries yield a more classic taste, similar to grape wine, while providing black cherry wine with a lovely dark red color. And Montmorency cherries are processed to create a lighter wine, pleasantly sour. Michigan grows 70 percent of the nation's tart cherries. Oregon and Washington are the next most prolific cherry producers. Michigan has done an excellent job of marketing itself as *the* cherry wine destination. But Door County is one of the few places on earth that make a chocolate cherry wine, which came close to making me believe in god.

It should be noted that Door County also features its share of wineries making wine from grapes. Wisconsin's grueling winters, cool springs, and pleasant summers actually provide the perfect conditions for the Frontenac, La Crescent, and Marquette grapes. Despite their French-sounding names, these hybrids were developed specifically for cold weather by the University of Minnesota in the current century. Coming down from the high of a weekend in Door County was mitigated by the case of cherry and grape wines we brought home. One of these was a wine called Frozen, a reference to Wisconsin winters, with a glib allusion to the wildly popular Disney movie also titled *Frozen*.

Saving wine culture may involve thinking less rigidly about what wine can be. Like apple wine, cherry wine offers a sustainable alternative to grape wine. Cherry wine does have a different life cycle from grape wine. Cherry wine should not be aged more than two years, and it is not as stable after bottling as grape wine. I would note, though, that technicians have been working on bottling grape wine for centuries, where cherry wine is a fledgling. It is possible, in other words, that the tech for bottling it just needs to catch up.

There are approximately fifty wineries making cherry wine in the United States. The Travis City, Michigan, media company notes, "These winemakers lend their training, experience, and expansive resources to perfecting—and experimenting with—the recipes pioneered in woodsheds, cellars, and kitchens" during the early days of American history, the Great Depression, and Prohibition.[35] The same site notes that it's common to see cherry trees growing alongside grape vineyards in Michigan. The state simultaneously produces red and white wines from grapes, especially Rieslings, Gewürztraminers, and Pinot Grigios.

The demand for cherry wine from Michigan is growing at an accelerated rate, atypical of the wine industry in general. The best example of this is perhaps Leelanau Cellars, where the winemakers and other staff have had to increase year-over-year production by 25 percent to keep up with demand. "Leelanau Cellars makes—and sells—36,000 bottles of gold medal-winning cherry wine per year," according to Cherrywine.[36] The nearby Chateau Grand Traverse makes six times that quantity. Twenty-first-century laws that permit wineries to ship out of state have also greatly helped small and regional wineries compete with larger companies.

What fruit wine skeptics may not understand is that cherry wine has tremendous versatility. It does *not* all taste the same. Sure, some of it is sweet, but any cherry winemaker worth her salt will also make a dry cherry table wine that pairs beautifully with food. Innovative vintners are also making a cherry port that comes in at approximately 20 percent alcohol through fortification with hard alcohol, often brandy. And then there's my favorite: dark chocolate dry cherry wine.

Of course, wine purists will complain that cherry winemakers add sugar to their mash, though it is generally not a substantial amount. This is needed to convert the juice to a level of alcohol content suitable for wine. Some cherry wine is only 8 percent alcohol. By adding sugar, winemakers can get it up to a 14 percent content that competes admirably with grape wine. Alternatives to sugar include honey and grape must. Though most cherry wine is aged in steel vats, some winemakers are experimenting with wood casks, especially oak. Clearly, the more thought that goes into the cask, the more complex and layered any wine will become.

If cherry wine is going to move out of the novelty tent and into the mainstream, winemakers will need to focus on making solid table wines and think about how cherry wine pairs with food. Many spokespeople on the subject will note that cherry wine goes well with Asian food and cheese, but all wine goes with Asian food and cheese. More drilling down, please.

One of the most astonishing things about cherry wine that I discovered while writing this book is how affordable both apple and cherry wines are. This is because the cost of raising cherries and apples is lower. Also, apples and cherries can be grown—and in fact flourish—in parts of the country where land is relatively cheap. By contrast, land in California is out of reach for most people who do not have several million dollars at their disposal.

Because cherry wine does not get aged beyond a few months in most cases, wineries can turn a profit more quickly and easily. This savings is inevitably passed to the consumer as price points are carefully examined. It is worth knowing that, in Canada, where the demand for cherry wine is greater, costs are more in line with the costs of grape wine. The cherry wine–loving Canadians are often willing to spend more for a good bottle of cherry wine than they pay for traditional grape wine. "Get drinking and enjoy the savings while prices are still so reasonable," Cherrywine advises.[37]

Conclusion

Return to Three Sisters

Come June of 2023, I left Louisville and returned to north Georgia and the A-frame cabin I bought in 2006. It needs substantial repairs. The deck is separating from the house, and the water pressure is so low, it takes twenty minutes to fill the small bathtub. The previous owners neglected to disclose the water damage to the subfloor. When I had the carpet pulled out, it became quite obvious that the floor is caving in, at several spots. It has no central heat or air, the cabinets are partly rotted, and all of the paneling needs to be replaced.

My neighbor, Dawn, has explained to me that my beloved cabin is a teardown. I don't have the expertise to know whether she is right or wrong. (Dawn likes to buy houses and tear them down.) I do worry that I could end up spending more than the house is worth to fix it. So, for the past three summers, I have been patching holes, painting, fighting mold, and trading out a few ugly appliances for better ones. The refrigerator roared for three summers, then quit working, so it really had to go.

I adore the mountains of Georgia, the winding roads, the lush green expanses, the wild orange azaleas, the mountain laurels, the lakes, the hiking trails, the funky little general stores that crop up in the middle of a forest. One sells pork barbecue and candles.

Joel put up two nectar feeders, and the hummingbirds swarmed us, performing winged ballet moves around our front and back decks all summer. All summer, I kept hoping to see a bottle of Fat Boy on a restaurant menu or in a gift store. The only retail store where I could find any Cynthiana was Mercier.

So Joel and I took the long and winding road to Dahlonega and Three Sisters. Motorcyclists call the stretch of two-lane blacktop leading from southeast Blue Ridge to Dahlonega "the dragon's tail." I'm a slow, careful driver, so a lot of the cyclists got impatient about passing us. I tried to slow down where they had a clear view of the road ahead.

Three Sisters was the same beautiful winery and vineyard that I remembered from earlier in the century. The three mountains after which it is named feature prominently in the background as one gazes at the grapevines marching up a hill.

Three Sisters owner Sharon Paul has had her own heartbreak in recent years. She lost her husband, Doug, in 2017. "We miss him every day!" she tells me in an email interview.[1]

I ask her why she and Doug chose to grow Cynthiana. She says, "This grape, *Vitis aestivalis*, is native to north Georgia. We have always embraced the history of the area. Especially where native American culture is concerned. We call it Cynthiana because Norton just does not sound very appealing (I put Norton in my computer to keep the bugs away). And with a name like Three Sisters, why would we *ever* call it Norton?"[2]

Doug and Sharon got their vines from Missouri. Considering the vineyard's output, I was amazed to learn that the Pauls started with only 6 acres, which they planted with Cynthiana. Today, they have 184 acres. "Our cultivation is twenty acres, consisting of both *vinifera* and indigenous grapes. We grow Cabernet Franc (the father of Cabernet Sauvignon), Chardonnay, Pinot Blanc, Vidal Blanc, and some new test varietals. Our largest planting is Cynthiana. We are proud to be Dahlonega's first family farm winery and the first 'legal' alcohol in Lumpkin County since prohibition," writes Paul.[3]

Three Sisters raises all the Cynthiana for their own five Cynthiana-based wines: Fat Boy Red, Cynthiana, Dry Rosé, Fat Boy's Chubby Cousin, and Joe Pye Dry. They also provide grapes to other producers. Fat Boy is by far their biggest seller. "We sell about three or four bottles of it to every one bottle of anything else. Cynthiana (the single varietal) is a favorite of big red drinkers . . . it's bold like a Malbec or Zinfandel," Paul says. She observes that *Vitis vinifera* is increasingly difficult to grow in north Georgia. Climate change is at least partly responsible. "Climate change is a real thing. Talk to any farmer!" Paul says, adding, "Colder cold and hotter hots are making diseases (and the bugs that bring them) harder to fight. Deer are rampant and voracious. Spring frosts (more likely freezes) hit hard in March and April."[4]

Planting a native vine sure did make a lot of sense. Cynthiana/Norton is difficult to get to maturity, but once established, it is hardier against the many grape-killing culprits that nature hands growers. It's my observation that Three Sisters does a better job of marketing wines locally than many other independent wineries. Nevertheless, I couldn't find it at Ingles, the most dominant grocery chain in north Georgia. So I ask Paul why people go to wines from California and Europe rather than buying locally.

She shoots the question back at me: "Please tell me if you can answer this!" It might come down to people erroneously thinking that all Georgia wine is sweet, Paul speculates. She's seeing a lot of "wonderful wines" made in Georgia, and they are not sweet. Like me, she wonders why the farm-to-table movement has not extended to wine.[5]

In the years since I last visited Three Sisters, I became very sick with a hereditary condition, underwent lifesaving surgery, spent a month in the hospital with postoperative complications, went on oxygen, lost my core strength, and had to relearn to walk with the help of some physical therapists.

I lost my taste for wine (and most food) for the three years that I was sick. But over time, I recovered not only my strength and love of life but also my love of good food and good wine. Returning to Three Sisters, after all those years, felt like a triumph—the end of a good book or summiting a mountain after a long climb. I never thought I would live this long; I never thought I would see that part of north Georgia again. But there I was.

The Fat Boy was just as delicious as I remembered, and I picked up more on notes of fig and chocolate, almost but not quite in competition with each other. Fat Boy is like a symphony. I can tell I'm not getting everything that's going on, so I just let it wash over me while I daydream a little. The label pictures an appropriately well-fed pig, and the winery cleverly refers to Fat Boy as a "swine wine."

I tasted a number of Cynthiana-based wines. There was a new one on the menu, called Joe Pye Dry. For the wine drinkers among my readership, I should immediately say that Joe Pye Dry is a great wine. Very dry, yes, but still flavorful and indelibly a Cynthiana. Three Sisters' marketing materials describe it as the dry version of Fat Boy. "Joe Pye is dedicated to Doug. It was his favorite wildflower. He always promoted it as our harbinger of harvest. It blooms in late summer," Sharon Paul tells me.[6]

Joel had some sticker shock from the prices at the winery—forty dollars for a single bottle in some cases. This puts a tentative finger on why it's not at the nearest supermarket. I know I will keep drinking Cynthiana/Norton, but I don't know how much. That, like the future of my A-frame, is one of life's uncertainties. The label on the Joe Pye Dry features a drawing of the lovely joe-pye weed with its pinkish, purplish blossoms, mushrooming above its long green stem. Joe-pye blooms all over north Georgia, feeding hummingbirds and a myriad of other wildlife, especially butterflies and other pollinators. It's a native plant taken largely for granted, often displaced in favor of more ornamental flowers and shrubs. But tree huggers like me love it.

Like the Cynthiana grape, joe-pye flourishes where it was born, a resource that we didn't even know to ask for. A blessing to those who drink from it.

GLOSSARY

biodiversity: A diversity of living plants, animals, and microorganisms that exist in stable relation to one another without species decline or loss. Agriculture and human habitations have historically displaced native plants and animals, leaving vineyard owners now needing to reintroduce native plants and animals in order to combat rising temperatures and drought.

Cabernet: A grape subspecies, originally from France and cultivated from *Vitis vinifera.* Two wines derived from the Cabernet grape are Cabernet Sauvignon and Cabernet Franc. Cabernet grapes are grown in many places in North America, but the California wine industry is closely associated with Cabernet, giving rise to the saying "Cabernet is king."

Cape of Good Hope grape: A grape cultivated from *Vitis labrusca* and grown by Jean Jacques Dufour, the first U.S. commercial winemaker.

Catawba craze: In the nineteenth century, the Catawba grape, a cultivar of *Vitis labrusca,* was the main ingredient in a very popular American sparkling wine. At the time, Catawba sparkling wine was compared favorably to French Champagne and even memorialized in a poem by Henry Wadsworth Longfellow.

Concord: A grape cultivated from *Vitis labrusca,* native to North America. This grape is extremely versatile and produces edible raw fruit—that is, table grapes. It is also an essential ingredient for grape juice, grape jam, grape jelly, and Concord wine.

Cynthiana (or Norton): A wine grape cultivated from *Vitis aestivalis* and hybridized with one or more of the *Vitis vinifera* grapes. Cynthiana has been reported as growing wild in the forests of Arkansas and Georgia.

fermentation: The process by which crushed grapes become wine and take on alcohol content. Fermentation is aided by choice of container, additives like yeast and sugar, and time.

fox: The musky or bitter edge to wild grapes that are native to North America, especially those cultivated from *Vitis labrusca.* According to wine critics, most wines made from *Vitis labrusca* are mildly to extremely "foxy."

hybridization: The act of grafting one grape species onto another or pollinating one grape with another grape species.

Muscadine: The common name for the *Vitis rotundifolia* grape as well as the juice and wine made from that grape.

Norton: *See* Cynthiana.

Norton's Virginia Seedling: The Norton grapevine that Dr. Daniel Norton cultivated commercially on his farm in Virginia.

Ohio River Valley: Shared by farming and winemaking regions in Ohio, Kentucky, Indiana, and Missouri, this valley features excellent soil that is good for growing food, especially grapes. It is frequently compared to the Rhine Valley in Germany.

phylloxera: An invasive, plant-eating insect that destroys grapevines. Originally, phylloxera traveled to Europe on grapevines imported from the United States. The phylloxera blight devastated wine grape crops across Europe, but grapes native to the United States were able to withstand the insect. To save the European wine industry, rootstock from native American grapes was grafted onto European grapevines.

Prohibition: *See* Volstead Act.

sustainability: A state of being that does not negatively impact the earth's or region's natural resources or climate. A vineyard becomes sustainable by rejecting tillage, conserving water, deploying alternative energy, planting native vegetation, and reintroducing or protecting native animals. A winery becomes sustainable by conserving water, using alternative energy, marketing locally, minimizing carbon emissions (especially as they relate to transportation), and reducing and recycling packaging materials where possible.

terroir: A French term for wine grape growing conditions; the particular soil, weather, and water that come together to make a wine that could only be made under those conditions. Connoisseurs believe you can taste the soil and water of a particular wine region in the wine itself.

varietal: A specific type of wine named after the subspecies of grape from which it is produced.

Vignoles: A wine grape widely grown in North America that tolerates a range of climates and soils very well. Originally thought to be French in origin, this grape turns out to be derived from at least two grapes cultivated by Albert Seibel, best known for experimenting with native American grape species.

viticulture: The science and methodology of winemaking, from figuring out how to grow grapes in available soil and weather, to hybridizing grapes, to fermenting grapes, to bottling and selling wine. This is a course of study offered at various universities.

***Vitis aestivalis*:** A grape species native to North America and the basis for Norton and Cynthiana wines.

***Vitis labrusca*:** A grape species native to North America and the basis for Concord grapes, as well as Alexander and Catawba wines.

***Vitis rotundifolia*:** A grape species native to North America and the basis for raw Muscadine grapes as well as Muscadine products, especially wine.

***Vitis rupestris*:** A grape species native to North America and known for durable rootstock. It is often grafted with more popular wine grapes to increase tolerance to heat and pests.

***Vitis vinifera*:** A grape species native to Europe, from which most European wines are derived. Burgundy, Cabernet, Rioja, Chianti, and Riesling, for example, are all derived from *vinifera*. It is also grown in Australia, California, Chile, Argentina, and South Africa, to name a few regions that have imported European grapes.

Volstead Act (or National Prohibition Act): In the United States, the Eighteenth Amendment, also called the Volstead Act, prevented the commercial sale of alcoholic beverages from 1920 to 1933. Because of loopholes and bootleggers, the act did little to curb drinking. However, it did disrupt the wine industry to the extent of destroying crops and winemaking equipment. Some historians believe that the American wine industry is still suffering the negative impacts of the Volstead Act.

NOTES

1. Fat Boy to Cynthiana

1. Zhu et al., "Phenolic Concentrations."
2. Zhu et al.
3. Roberts, *From This Hill*, 19.

2. Origins of Cynthiana

1. Kliman, *Wild Vine*, 28.
2. Warwick, *Warwick's Keystone Commonwealth*, 240.
3. Kliman, *Wild Vine*, 23.
4. Kliman, 56.
5. Kliman, 56.
6. Kliman, 381.
7. Norton, "On Foreign and Native Grapes," 589.
8. Norton, 590.
9. Kliman, *Wild Vine*, 58–59.
10. Kenrick, *New American Orchardist*, 259.
11. Kenrick, 259.
12. Kenrick, 259.
13. Kliman, *Wild Vine*, 61.
14. Stover et al., "Investigations."
15. Lapsley, "Wine in America."
16. Hedrick, *Grapes of New York*, 227.
17. Gibbs, "Wines and Vines," 586.
18. Gibbs, 587.
19. Gibbs, 589.
20. Roberts, *From This Hill*, 110.
21. Münch, *School for American Grape Culture*, 11.
22. Pinney, *History of Wine*, 180.
23. Pinney, 175.
24. Kliman, *Wild Vine*, 91.

25. Kliman, 90–92.
26. Pinney, *History of Wine*, 176.
27. Pinney, 105.
28. Husmann, "Future of Grape Growing," 237.
29. Husmann, 109.
30. Husmann, 176.
31. Kliman, *Wild Vine*, 110.
32. Poeschel, "Letter to the Western Journal," 54–55.
33. Poeschel, 55.
34. Poeschel, 55.
35. Poeschel, 55.
36. Poeschel, 113.
37. Husmann, *Grape Culturist*, 97–99.
38. Goodspeed and Snider, *History of Franklin, Jefferson, Washington*, 1119.
39. Little, "How Prohibition Fueled."
40. Kliman, *Wild Vine*, 154.
41. McKee, "Missouri Wine Pioneer."
42. Kliman, *Wild Vine*, [illegible].
43. McKee, "Missouri Wine Pioneer."
44. Lapsley, "Wine in America."

3. Where's the Wine?

1. Koci, "First Commercial Winery."
2. Pinney, *History of Wine*.
3. Koci, "First Commercial Winery."
4. Feinstein, "Understanding Alluvial Soils."
5. Ksander, "Wine Production."
6. Clark, *Kentucky*.
7. Westrich, "French Wine Makers."
8. Clark, *Kentucky*.
9. Koci, "First Commercial Winery."
10. Clark, *Kentucky*.
11. Clay, *Papers of Henry Clay*, 594.
12. Pinney, *History of Wine*.
13. Pinney, 122.
14. Pinney, 125.
15. Butler and Butler, *Indiana Wine*, 70.
16. Pinney, *History of Wine*, 146.
17. Pinney, 157–59.
18. Pinney, 161.
19. Longfellow, *Poems*, 159.
20. Fauchald, "Father of American Sparkling Wine."

21. Menderski, "Civil War Battle."
22. Kentuckians for the Commonwealth, "Indigenous Lands Acknowledgement."
23. Kent, "European Colonizers Killed."
24. Harrison and Klotter, *New History of Kentucky*, 214.
25. Jackson, "Work of the Anti-Saloon League," 16.
26. Burns and Novick, *Prohibition*.
27. Burns and Novick.
28. Schrad, "Hatchet Nation."
29. Scovell, "President's Address."
30. Scovell.
31. Okrent, *Last Call*.
32. Moore, *Citizen Klansmen*, 191.
33. Laskow, "For Sale."
34. Bureau of Alcohol, Tobacco, Firearms and Explosives, "Frank A. Mather."
35. Burns and Novick, *Prohibition*.
36. Chesak, "How One Kentucky Town."
37. Koop, "Fact—Cigarettes Kill."
38. Inman, "Hard Pressed."
39. Quinones, "I Don't Know."
40. Calling All Contestants, "Wildside Winery."

4. Hermann Rises Again

1. Rodriguez, "Cynthiana (Norton) Grape."
2. Adam Puchta Winery, "Story."
3. CBS, "How Morley Safer."
4. UC Davis, "Vignoles."
5. UC Davis.
6. Lady Bird Johnson Wildflower Center, "*Vitis aestivalis* var. *Lincecumii*."
7. Held interview.
8. McKee, "Missouri Wine Pioneer."
9. Kliman, *Wild Vine*, 168.
10. Kliman, 172–73.
11. Kliman, 175.
12. Kliman, 184.
13. Asher, *Vineyard Tales*, 40.
14. Kliman, *Wild Vine*, 198.
15. Scala, "Dennis Horton."
16. McIntyre, "Man Who Turned."
17. Scala, "Dennis Horton."
18. McIntyre, "Man Who Turned."
19. McIntyre.
20. Roberts interview.

21. Cheney, “She’s Just Wild.”
22. Wine Enthusiast, “Plant Something Native.”
23. Cheney, “She’s Just Wild.”
24. Wine Enthusiast, “Plant Something Native.”
25. Cheney, “She’s Just Wild.”
26. Cheney.
27. Cheney.
28. McCloud interview.
29. McCloud interview.
30. Wine Enthusiast, “Plant Something Native.”
31. McCloud interview.
32. McCloud interview.
33. McCloud interview.
34. McCloud interview.
35. McCloud interview.
36. McCloud interview.
37. McCloud interview.

5. The Cult of Cynthiana

1. Chateau Aux Arc, “About Us.”
2. Chateau Aux Arc.
3. Chateau Aux Arc.
4. Wilson, “Air Conditioning.”
5. Post interview.
6. Post interview.
7. Post interview.
8. Post interview.
9. Post interview.
10. Post interview.
11. Post interview.
12. Post interview.
13. Post interview.
14. Post interview.
15. Post interview.
16. Post interview.

6. The Screaming Canary

1. Barber, “Climate Change Means.”
2. Johnson-Bell, *Wine and Climate Change*, 42.
3. Johnson-Bell, vii.
4. Johnson-Bell, 115.
5. Sanderson, “Azienda Agricola Valentini.”

6. Valentini and Di Carlo, "Advance of Grape Harvest."
7. Valentini and Di Carlo.
8. Millan, "Climate Change Linked."
9. Hersher, "You've Likely Been Affected."
10. Willsher, "French Winemakers Count Cost."
11. Givetash, "Climate Change Makes."
12. Givetash.
13. Nesbitt et al., "Climate Change Projections."
14. Givetash, "Climate Change Makes."
15. Freedman, *Crushed*, 69.
16. Selinger, "In England, Varied Soils."
17. Freedman, *Crushed*, 69.
18. Freedman, 72.
19. Flavelle, "Scorched, Parched."
20. Flavelle.
21. Chipman, "California's $45 Billion."
22. Savage, "Why California's $46 Billion?"
23. Carl, "Local Tastes."
24. Bartlett interview.
25. Bartlett interview.
26. Bartlett interview.
27. Bartlett interview.
28. Freedman, *Crushed*.
29. Eligon, "Exploring South Africa's."
30. Freedman, *Crushed*, 157.
31. USAID, "South Africa Climate Change."
32. Frost, "Fire and Ice."
33. Environmental and Energy Study Institute, "Climate Change FAQ."
34. Graham, "No-Till Farming."
35. Graham.
36. Graham.
37. Prieur, "Could No-Till Farming?"
38. Prieur.
39. Graham, "No-Till Farming."
40. Prieur, "Could No-Till Farming?"
41. Todd, "Woman Who Started."
42. Freedman, *Crushed*, 45–47.
43. Todd, "Woman Who Started."
44. Freedman, *Crushed*, 49.
45. Rosane, "Planting Billions of Trees."
46. Marshall, "Planting Trees."
47. Roth, "Parducci's Sustainability Journey."

48. Mendocino Wine Company, *Parducci's.*
49. Burzynska, "Going Green."
50. *Dish,* "What Sustainability Looks Like."
51. *Dish.*
52. Johnson-Bell, *Wine and Climate Change,* 104.
53. Familia Torres, "Beyond Sustainability."
54. Desimone, "Amid Climate Change."
55. Desimone.
56. Familia Torres, "Bodegas Torres Reintroduces Moneu."
57. Familia Torres.
58. Carl, "Local Tastes."
59. Carl.
60. Johnson-Bell, *Wine and Climate Change,* 79.
61. Johnson-Bell, 78.

7. Must Wine Be Grape?

1. Mayyasi, "Why Is Wine (Almost)?"
2. *Wine Spectator,* "Why Are Grapes So Much?"
3. Tannin Food Intolerance, "Food and Drinks."
4. Schneider, *Wine for Normal People,* 12.
5. Schneider, 12.
6. Schneider, 34.
7. Tobias, "Best Non-grape Fruit Wines."
8. Klimek, "Nectar of the Gods."
9. McGovern, "Prehistoric China."
10. Gratzer, "Challenges and Perspectives."
11. Minnick, *Mead.*
12. Minnick, 112.
13. Minnick, 178.
14. Minnick, 182.
15. Minnick, 179.
16. Richmond, *From Da to Yes,* 69.
17. Minnick, *Mead,* 148.
18. Klimek, "Nectar of the Gods."
19. Minnick, "Mead."
20. Rehagen, "Mead Has a Long History."
21. Rehagen.
22. Rehagen.
23. Borenstein, "Nearly Half."
24. Hall, "Mead Is Trendy Again."
25. Kerrigan, *Johnny Appleseed,* 19.

26. Jiménez-Pavón et al., "Effects of a Moderate Intake." See also Wijnen et al., "Post-Exercise Rehydration."
27. Ginzburg, "Harvest Is In."
28. Means, *Johnny Appleseed*, 11.
29. Pollan, "Botany of Desire."
30. Geiling, "Real Johnny Appleseed."
31. PBS, "Ernest Gallo."
32. Singer, "Sweet Wine of Youth."
33. Russell, "Taxing Vices."
34. Smith, "Untold Truth."
35. Cherrywine, "Cherry Wine Story."
36. Cherrywine.
37. Cherrywine.

Conclusion

1. Paul interview.
2. Paul interview.
3. Paul interview.
4. Paul interview.
5. Paul interview.
6. Paul interview.

BIBLIOGRAPHY

Adam Puchta Winery. "Story." Accessed May 8, 2024. https://adampuchtawine.com/story/.

Asher, Gerald. *Vineyard Tales: Reflections on Wine*. San Francisco: Chronicle, 1996.

Barber, Elizabeth. "Climate Change Means Soft and Sour Apples." *Christian Science Monitor*, August 15, 2013. https://www.csmonitor.com/Science/2013/0815/Climate-change-means-soft-and-sour-apples-study-finds.

Bartlett, Megan. Author interview, October 6, 2023.

Borenstein, Seth. "Nearly Half of US Honeybee Colonies Died Last Year." Associated Press, June 22, 2023. https://apnews.com/article/honeybees-pollinator-extinct-disease-death-climate-change-f60297706e19c7346ff1881587b5aced.

Bureau of Alcohol, Tobacco, Firearms and Explosives. "Frank A. Mather." Accessed May 8, 2023. https://www.atf.gov/our-history/fallen-agents/frank-mather.

Burns, Ken, and Lynn Novick, dirs. *Prohibition*. PBS, 2011.

Burzynska, Jo. "Going Green." *New Zealand Herald*, May 9, 2009.

Butler, J. L., and J. J. Butler. *Indiana Wine: A History*. Bloomington: Indiana University Press, 2001.

Calling All Contestants. "Wildside Winery." Accessed May 8, 2024. https://callingallcontestants.com/directory/wildside-winery/.

Carl, Tim. "Local Tastes: The 2023 Outlook." *Napa Valley Register*, June 22, 2023. https://napavalleyregister.com/wine/columnists/tim-carl/tim-carl-local-tastes-the-2023-outlook-brutal-for-the-wine-indstry-but-good-for/article_5cc510ac-8bc9-11ed-93f3-17073bf3557a.html.

CBS. "How Morley Safer Convinced Americans to Drink More Wine." August 28, 2016. https://www.cbsnews.com/news/how-morley-safer-convinced-americans-to-drink-more-wine/.

Chateau Aux Arc. "About Us." Accessed May 8, 2024. https://chateauauxarc.com/about-us.

Cheney, Catherine. "She's Just Wild about Norton." *Washington Post*, September 9, 2009. https://www.washingtonpost.com/wp-dyn/content/article/2009/09/08/AR2009090800991.html.

Cherrywine. "Cherry Wine Story." Accessed May 8, 2023. https://cherrywine.com/learn-about/cherry-wines/.

Chesak, Chez. "How One Kentucky Town Almost Became Vegas." *Los Angeles Times*, August 3, 2019. https://www.latimes.com/travel/story/2019-08-02/newport-kentucky-las-vegas-gambling-big-name-stars-mob.

Chipman, Kim. "California's $45 Billion Wine Industry Faces Climate Peril." Bloomberg, September 7, 2022. https://www.bloomberg.com/news/articles/2022-09-07/california-s-wine-industry-faces-climate-tipping-point.

Clark, Thomas D. *The Kentucky*. Lexington: University Press of Kentucky, 2021.

Clay, H. *The Papers of Henry Clay: The Rising Statesman, 1797–1814*. Lexington: University Press of Kentucky, 2014.

Desimone, Mike. "Amid Climate Change, Spain's Torres Family Bets on Ancient Grapes." Wine Enthusiast, May 31, 2023. https://www.wineenthusiast.com/culture/familia-torres/.

Dish. "What Sustainability Looks Like to a Winemaker with Esme Holdsworth from Grove Mill." November 12, 2020. https://dish.co.nz/drinks/news/what-sustainability-looks-winemaker-esme-holdsworth-grove-mill/.

Eligon, John. "Exploring South Africa's Black Wine Scene." *New York Times*, February 15, 2023. https://www.nytimes.com/2023/02/15/travel/black-south-african-wine.html.

Environmental and Energy Study Institute. "Climate Change FAQ." Accessed February 19, 2021. https://www.eesi.org/files/FactSheet_Climate_Change_FAQ_2021.pdf.

Familia Torres. "Beyond Sustainability." Accessed May 9, 2023. https://www.torres.es/en/beyond-sustainability.

———. "Bodegas Torres Reintroduces Moneu." June 1, 2016. https://www.torres.es/en/news/bodegas-torres-reintroduces-moneu-ancestral-red-grape-penedes.

Fauchald, Nick. "The Father of American Sparkling Wine." *Wine Spectator*, June 28, 2024. https://www.winespectator.com/articles/the-father-of-american-sparkling-wine-2133.

Feinstein, Laura. "Understanding Alluvial Soils in Wine." Wine Enthusiast, September 29, 2022. www.wineenthusiast.com/basics/advanced-studies/alluvial-soils-wine/.

Flavelle, Christopher. "Scorched, Parched and Now Uninsurable." *San Francisco Examiner*, July 19, 2021. https://www.sfexaminer.com/archives/scorched-parched-and-now-uninsurable-climate-change-hits-wine-country/article_536c8b19-6bde-5f90-aba5-c4c90df0d8c9.html.

———. "They're Putting Sunscreen on Grapes in California's Wine Country." *New York Times*, July 18, 2021. https://www.nytimes.com/live/2021/07/20/us/climate-heat-wildfires#california-wine-country.

Freedman, B. *Crushed: How a Changing Climate Is Altering the Way We Drink*. London: Rowman & Littlefield, 2022.

Frost, Robert. "Fire and Ice." Poetry Foundation, accessed May 8, 2024. https://www.poetryfoundation.org/poems/44263/fire-and-ice.

Geiling, Natasha. "The Real Johnny Appleseed." *Smithsonian Magazine*, November 10, 2014. https://www.smithsonianmag.com/arts-culture/real-johnny-appleseed-brought-applesand-booze-american-frontier-180953263/.

Gibbs, John. "Wines and Vines in the Old Dominion." *Southern Bivouac*, Southern Historical Association of Louisville, March 1887. https://www.google.com/books/edition/

The_Southern_Bivouac/-f-7TmDw89kC?hl=en&gbpv=1&dq=Gibbs,+John.+%E2%80%9CWines+and+Vines+in+the+Old+Dominion.%E2%80%9D+The+Southern+Bivouac.+United+States:+Southern+Historical+Association+of+Louisville.+1887.&pg=PA589&printsec=frontcover.

Ginzburg, Ralph. "Harvest Is in at Centuries-Old Distillery." *New York Times*, October 26, 1986. https://www.nytimes.com/1986/10/26/nyregion/harvest-is-in-at-centuries-old-distillery.html.

Givetash, Linda. "Climate Change Makes England's Vineyards Perfect for Sparkling Wine." NBC, February 23, 2019. https://www.nbcnews.com/news/world/climate-change-makes-england-s-vineyards-perfect-sparkling-wine-n962606.

Goodspeed, Weston Arthur, and Felix E. Snider. *History of Franklin, Jefferson, Washington, Crawford and Gasconade Counties, Missouri: From the Earliest Time to the Present; Together with Sundry Personal, Business and Professional Sketches and Numerous Family Records; Besides a Valuable Fund of Notes, Original Observations*. Chicago: Goodspeed, 1888.

Graham, Lester. "No-Till Farming Could Cut Greenhouse Gasses Significantly." Michigan Radio, accessed November 12, 2019. https://www.michiganradio.org/environment-science/2019-11-12/no-till-farming-could-cut-greenhouse-gases-significantly.

Gratzer, Kristina. "Challenges and Perspectives for Beekeeping in Ethiopia." Accessed June 29, 2021, https://link.springer.com/article/10.1007/s13593-021-00702-2.

Hall, Mary. "Mead Is Trendy Again." News Nation Now, April 26, 2023. https://www.newsnationnow.com/climate/mead-trendy-again-help-save-honey-bees/.

Harrison, L. H., and J. C. Klotter. *A New History of Kentucky*. Lexington: University Press of Kentucky, 1997.

Hersher, Rebecca. "You've Likely Been Affected by Climate Change." NPR, June 21, 2022. https://www.npr.org/2022/06/21/1102389274/climate-change-costs-extreme-weather.

Husmann, George. *The Cultivation of the Native Grape, and Manufacture of American Wines*. New York: Geo. E. & F. W. Woodward, 1866.

———. "Future of Grape Growing in the West." In *The Missouri Yearbook of Agriculture: Annual Report*, 237. Jefferson City: Missouri State Board of Agriculture, 1878.

———, ed. *The Grape Culturist*. St. Louis MO: Geo. H. Husmann, 1871.

Hedrick, U. P. *The Grapes of New York*. Czechia: Good Press, 2021.

Held, Nathan. Author interview, May 11, 2023.

Heming, Carol. "George Husmann 1827–1902." *Missouri Encyclopedia*, State Historical Society of Virginia, 1999. https://missouriencyclopedia.org/people/husmann-george.

Inman, Taylor. "Hard Pressed: Kentucky Winery Owners Feel Stifled." WKMS, November 13, 2018. https://www.wkms.org/business-economy/2018-11-13/hard-pressed-ky-winery-owners-feel-stifled-by-caps-on-production.

Jackson, J. C. "The Work of the Anti-Saloon League." *Annals of the American Academy of Political and Social Science* 32 (November 1908). https://www.jstor.org/stable/1010548.

Jiménez-Pavón, David, Mónica Sofía Cervantes-Borunda, Ligia Esperanza Díaz, Ascensión Marcos, and Manuel J. Castillo. "Effects of a Moderate Intake of Beer on Markers of Hydration after Exercise in the Heat: A Crossover Study." *Journal of International*

Society of Sports Nutrition 12 (2015): 26. https://www.ncbi.nlm.nih.gov/pmc/articles/PMC4459073/.

Johnson-Bell, L. *Wine and Climate Change*. Ithaca NY: Burford, 2014.

Kenrick, W. *The New American Orchardist: or, An Account of the Most Valuable Varieties of Fruit, of All Climates, Adapted to Cultivation in the United States; with Their History, Modes of Culture, Management, Uses, &c. With an Appendix on Vegetables, Ornamental Trees, Shrubs, and Flowers, the Agricultural Resources of America, and on Silk, &c.* Bedford MA: Otis, Broaders, 1844.

Kent, Lauren. "European Colonizers Killed So Many Native Americans That It Changed the Global Climate." CNN, February 2, 2019. https://www.cnn.com/2019/02/01/world/european-colonization-climate-change-trnd/index.html.

Kentuckians for the Commonwealth. "Indigenous Lands Acknowledgement." Accessed May 10, 2023. https://archive.kftc.org/indigenous-lands-acknowledgment.

Kerrigan, William. *Johnny Appleseed and the American Orchard: A Cultural History*. Baltimore: Johns Hopkins University Press, 2012.

Kliman, Todd. *The Wild Vine: A Forgotten Grape and the Untold Story of American Wine*. New York: Crown, 2011.

Klimek, Chris. "The Nectar of the Gods Is Coming to a Bar near You." *Smithsonian Magazine*, September–October 2023. https://www.smithsonianmag.com/arts-culture/nectar-gods-mead-bar-meadery-180982702/.

Koci, Petra. "The First Commercial Winery in the United States." Swiss National Museum, 2023. https://blog.nationalmuseum.ch/en/2022/08/dufours-wine-business-in-america/.

Koop, C. Everett. "Fact—Cigarettes Kill More People per Year Than AIDS." National Library of Medicine, 1989. https://collections.nlm.nih.gov/catalog/nlm:nlmuid-101450285-img.

Ksander, Yaël. "Wine Production." Indiana Public Media, 2008. https://indianapublicmedia.org/momentofindianahistory/wine-production/.

Lady Bird Johnson Wildflower Center. "*Vitis aestivalis* var. *Lincecumii*." Accessed November 1, 2022. https://www.wildflower.org/plants/result.php?id_plant=VIAEL.

Lapsley, Jim. "Wine in America." PBS, 2017. https://www.pbs.org/wgbh/americanexperience/features/wine-america/.

Laskow, Sarah. "For Sale: Pre-Prohibition Whiskey." *Atlas Obscura*, December 3, 2018. https://www.atlasobscura.com/articles/pre-prohibition-whiskey-for-sale.

Little, Becky. "How Prohibition Fueled the Rise of the Ku Klux Klan." History, October 16, 2023. www.history.com/news/kkk-terror-during-prohibition.

Longfellow, Henry Wadsworth. *Poems of Henry Wadsworth Longfellow*. New York: Thomas Y. Crowell, 1901.

Marshall, Michael. "Planting Trees Doesn't Always Help with Climate Change." BBC, May 26, 2020. https://www.bbc.com/future/article/20200521-planting-trees-doesnt-always-help-with-climate-change.

Mayyasi, Alex. "Why Is Wine (Almost) Always Made from Grapes?" *Atlas Obscura*, June 6, 2022. https://www.atlasobscura.com/articles/why-is-wine-made-from-grapes.

McCloud, Jennifer. Author interview, October 25, 2023.

McGovern, Patrick. "Prehistoric China." Pennsylvania Museum, accessed May 11, 2023. https://www.penn.museum/sites/biomoleculararchaeology/resources/ancient-china/.

McIntyre, Dave. "The Man Who Turned Underdog Grapes into Virginia's Star Wines." *Washington Post*, June 22, 2018. https://www.washingtonpost.com/lifestyle/food/he-turned-underdog-grapes-into-virginias-star-wines/2018/06/21/a9be3432-758b-11e8-805c-4b67019fcfe4_story.html.

McKee, Linda Jones. "Missouri Wine Pioneer Jim Held Dies." *Wine Business*, October 2023. www.winebusiness.com/news/article/222264.

Means, Howard. *Johnny Appleseed: The Man, the Myth, the American Story*. New York: Simon & Schuster, 2012.

Menderski, Amanda. "A Civil War Battle." *Courier Journal*, January 21, 2021.

Mendocino Wine Company. *Parducci's Green Winegrowing Handbook*. Ukiah CA: Mendocino Wine Company, 2008.

Millan, Laura. "Climate Change Linked to 5 Million Deaths a Year." Bloomberg, accessed July 7, 2021. https://www.bloomberg.com/news/articles/2021-07-07/climate-change-linked-to-5-million-deaths-a-year-new-study-shows?embedded-checkout=true.

Minnick, Fred. *Mead: The Libations, Legends, and Lore of History's Oldest Drink*. Philadelphia: Running Press, 2018.

———. "Mead: The Return of the Sweet, Ancient Flavor." *Forbes*, November 28, 2018. https://www.forbes.com/sites/fredminnick/2018/11/28/mead-the-return-of-the-sweet-ancient-flavor/?sh=1135b0101967.

Moore, L. J. *Citizen Klansmen: The Ku Klux Klan in Indiana, 1921–1928*. Chapel Hill: University of North Carolina Press, 1997.

Münch, F. *School for American Grape Culture: Brief but Thorough and Practical Guide to the Laying Out of Vineyards, the Treatment of Vines, and the Production of Wine in North America*. St. Louis MO: C. Witter, 1865.

Nesbitt, A., S. Dorling, R. Jones, D. K. Smith, M. Krumins, K. E. Gannon, and D. Conway. "Climate Change Projections for UK Viticulture to 2040: A Focus on Improving Suitability for Pinot Noir." *OENO One* 56, no. 3 (July 2022): 69–87. https://oeno-one.eu/article/view/5398.

Nick, Fauchald. "The Father of American Sparkling Wine." *Wine Spectator*, June 28, 2004. https://www.winespectator.com/articles/the-father-of-american-sparkling-wine-2133.

Norton, Daniel. "On Foreign and Native Grapes." In *The Farmers' Register: A Monthly Publication Devoted to the Improvement of the Practice, and Support of the Interests of Agriculture*, 520. Shellbanks VA: Edmund Ruffin, 1834. https://www.google.com/books/edition/The_Farmers_Register/mfBQAAAAYAAJ?hl=en&gbpv=1&bsq=Norton,%20Daniel.

Okrent, Daniel. *Last Call: The Rise and Fall of Prohibition*. London: Scribner, 2010.

———. "Wayne B. Wheeler: The Man Who Turned Off the Taps." *Smithsonian Magazine*, May 2010. https://www.smithsonianmag.com/history/wayne-b-wheeler-the-man-who-turned-off-the-taps-14783512/.

Paul, Sharon. Author interview, October 12, 2023.

PBS. "Ernest Gallo." Accessed May 9, 2023. https://www.pbs.org/wgbh/pages/frontline/president/players/gallo.html.

Pennsylvania Wine School. "What Is a Vignoles?" Accessed September 24, 2018. https://pennsylvaniawine.com/wine-education/blog/pennsylvania-grapes-guide#:~:text=VIGNOLES%20(veen%2DYOL)%20is,%2Dlike%20full%2Dbodied%20wine.

Pinney, Thomas. *A History of Wine in America*. Vol. 1, *From the Beginnings to Prohibition*. Berkeley: University of California Press, 1989.

Poeschel, Michael. "Letter to the Western Journal." In *Western Journal, and Civilian: Devoted to Agriculture, Manufactures, Mechanic Arts, Internal Improvement, Commerce, Public Policy, and Polite Literature*. N.p.: Charles & Hammond, 1850. https://www.google.com/books/edition/The_Western_Journal_and_Civilian/vhQ6AQAAMAAJ?hl=en&gbpv=1&bsq=Poeschel.

Pollan, Michael. "Botany of Desire." MichaelPollan.com, accessed June 29, 2001. https://michaelpollan.com/interviews/botany-of-desire/.

Post, Tina. Author interview, October 10, 2023.

Prieur, Danielle. "Could No-Till Farming Reverse Climate Change?" *U.S. News*, August 4, 2016. https://www.usnews.com/news/articles/2016-08-04/could-no-till-farming-reverse-climate-change.

Quinones, Sam. "I Don't Know That I Would Even Call It Meth Anymore." *Atlantic Monthly*, October 18, 2021. https://www.theatlantic.com/magazine/archive/2021/11/the-new-meth/620174/.

Rehagen, Tony. "Mead Has a Long History and a Future as a Sustainable Beer Alternative." *Washington Post*, August 14, 2023. https://www.washingtonpost.com/food/2023/08/10/mead-sustainability-beer-alternative/.

Richmond, Y. *From Da to Yes: Understanding the East Europeans*. London: Intercultural, 1995.

Roberts, Paul. Author interview, October 24, 2023.

———. *From This Hill, My Hand, Cynthiana Wine*. N.p.: Resonant, 1999.

Rodriguez, Jeronimo. "Cynthiana (Norton) Grape Cultivar's DNA Fingerprinting—a Ninety-Year-Old Mystery Solved." ResearchGate, accessed October 2023. https://www.researchgate.net/publication/374545123_Cynthiana_Norton_grape_cultivar's_DNA_fingerprinting-a_190_year-old_mystery_solved.

Rosane, Olivia. "Planting Billions of Trees Is the 'Best Climate Change Solution Available Today.'" Ecowatch, July 5, 2019. https://www.ecowatch.com/climate-change-planting-trees-2639092782.html.

Roth, Patricia. "Parducci's Sustainability Journey Brings Esteemed Environmental Award." *Wine Business*, October 1, 2009. https://www.winebusiness.com/news/article/67938.

Russell, Cristine. "Taxing Vices." *Washington Post*, October 30, 1990. https://www.washingtonpost.com/archive/lifestyle/wellness/1990/10/30/taxing-vices/d18830b0-4921-425d-93de-e1797aecb0a0/.

Sanderson, Bruce. "Azienda Agricola Valentini: An Enigma in Abruzzo." *Wine Spectator*, June 18, 2010. https://www.winespectator.com/articles/azienda-agricola-valentini-an-enigma-in-abruzzo-42961.

Savage, Steven. "Why California's $46 Billion Wine Industry Is Better Prepared for Climate Change Than Some of Its Competitors?" *Forbes*, November 29, 2022. https://www.forbes.com/sites/stevensavage/2022/11/29/why-californias-46-billion-wine-industry-is-better-prepared-for-climate-change-than-some-of-its-competitors/?sh=27ea1ae27096.

Scala, Erin. "Dennis Horton Was an Innovative Pioneer." *C-ville Weekly*, June 27, 2018. https://www.c-ville.com/dennis-horton-innovative-pioneer-virginia-wine/.

Schneider, Elizabeth. *Wine for Normal People: A Guide for Real People Who Like Wine, but Not the Snobbery That Goes with It*. San Francisco: Chronicle, 2019.

Schrad, Mark Lawrence. "Hatchet Nation." *Slate*, September 7, 2021. https://slate.com/news-and-politics/2021/09/carry-nation-biography-reasons-for-activism.html.

Scovell, Bessie Laythe. "President's Address." In *Minutes of the Twenty-Fourth Annual Meeting of the W.C.T.U. of the State of Minnesota*. St. Paul: W. J. Woodbury, 1900. https://speakingwhilefemale.co/temperance-scovell/.

Selinger, Hannah. "In England, Varied Soils Meet Cool-Climate Winemakng." Wine Enthusiast, May 8, 2023. https://www.wineenthusiast.com/basics/england-wine-guide-sparkling/.

Singer, Mark. "Sweet Wine of Youth." *Esquire*, June 1, 1972. https://classic.esquire.com/article/1972/6/1/sweet-wine-of-youth.

Smith, Crawford. "The Untold Truth of Boone's Farm." Mashed, accessed September 22, 2021. https://www.mashed.com/612503/the-untold-truth-of-boones-farm/.

Stover, E., M. Aradhya, J. Yang, J. Bautista, and G. S. Dangle. "Investigations into the Origin of 'Norton' Grape Using SSR Markers." *Proceedings of Florida State Horticultural Society* 122 (2010): 19–24. https://www.researchgate.net/profile/Ed-Stover/publication/44019160_Investigations_into_the_Origin_of_%27Norton%27_Grape_using_SSR_Markers/links/54930fe80cf286fe31240116/Investigations-into-the-Origin-of-Norton-Grape-using-SSR-Markers.pdf.

Tannin Food Intolerance. "Food and Drinks That Contain Tannin." Accessed May 8, 2024. https://tanninfoodintolerance.org/food-and-drinks-that-contain-tannin/.

Tobias, Ruth. "Best Non-grape Fruit Wines." Tasting Table, accessed February 14, 2022. https://www.tastingtable.com/690757/fruit-wine-cherry-wine-apple-wine-chateau-fontaine-maui-winery/.

Todd, Cathrine. "The Woman Who Started a Viticulture Revolution in Israel." *Forbes*, July 30, 2019. https://www.forbes.com/sites/cathrinetodd/2019/07/30/the-woman-who-started-a-viticulture-revolution-in-israel/?sh=2e5192223a3f.

UC Davis. "Vignoles." Accessed May 8, 2024. https://fps.ucdavis.edu/fgrdetails.cfm?varietyid=2808.

USAID. "South Africa Climate Change Country Profile." Accessed November 15, 2022. https://www.usaid.gov/climate/country-profiles/south-africa.

Valentini, Francesco Paolo, and Piero Di Carlo. "Advance of Grape Harvest Date of a Premium Wine in Central Italy." *Ciencia & Vinho*, June 30, 2019. https://www.ciencia-e-vinho.com/2019/06/30/advance-of-grape-harvest-date-of-a-premium-wine-in-central-italy-evidence-of-the-role-of-precipitation-intensity-under-a-warming-climate/.

Warwick, C. F. *Warwick's Keystone Commonwealth: A Review of the History of the Great State of Pennsylvania, and a Brief Record of the Growth of Its Chief City, Philadelphia*. Philadelphia: Ella K. Warwick, 1913.

Westrich, Sal. “French Wine Makers and the Launching of American Viticulture.” American Association of Wine Economists, 2016. https://wine-economics.org/wp-content/uploads/2016/10/AAWE_WP207.pdf.

Wijnen, H. C., Jora Steennis Annemarthe, Milène Catoire, Floris C. Wardenaar, and Marco Mensink. “Post-Exercise Rehydration: Effect of Consumption of Beer with Varying Alcohol Content on Fluid Balance after Mild Dehydration.” PubMed, 2016. https://www.frontiersin.org/articles/10.3389/fnut.2016.00045/full.

Willsher, Kim. “French Winemakers Count Cost of Devastating Hailstorms.” *Guardian*, August 9, 2013. https://www.theguardian.com/world/2013/aug/09/bordeaux-wine-vineyards-hailstorms-damage.

Wilson, Eric Dean. “Air Conditioning Will Not Save Us.” *Time*, July 22, 2022. https://time.com/6199353/air-conditioning-will-not-save-us/.

Wine Enthusiast. “Plant Something Native.” September 20, 2022. https://www.wineenthusiast.com/culture/industry-news/plant-something-native-5-questions-with-jenni-mccloud/.

Wine Spectator. “Why Are Grapes So Much More Popular for Making Wine Than Other Fruits?” March 23, 2020. https://www.winespectator.com/articles/why-are-grapes-so-much-more-popular-for-making-wine-than-other-fruits.

Zhu, L., Y. Zhang, J. Deng, H. Li, and J. Lu. “Phenolic Concentrations and Antioxidant Properties of Wines Made from North American Grapes Grown in China.” *Molecules* 17, no. 3 (2012): 3304–23. https://www.ncbi.nlm.nih.gov/pmc/articles/PMC6268268/.